The Five Divorces of a Healthy Marriage

Experiencing the Stages of Love

by Harold Straughn

CBP Press
St. Louis, Missouri

Unless otherwise indicated, all scripture quotations are from the
Revised Standard Version of the Bible, copyrighted 1946, 1952, © 1971,
1973, by the Division of Christian Education of the National Council of
the Churches of Christ in the United States of America, and are used by
permission.

Library of Congress Cataloging in Publication Data
Straughn, Harold.
    The Five Divorces of a Healthy Marriage
    1. Marriage—History. 2. Love—History. 3—Interpersonal rela-
tions—History. 4. Life cycle, Human. I. Title.
HQ728.S857   1986   306.8'1   85-29923
ISBN 0-8272-2318-8

Printed in the United States of America

Contents

1. Conversion
2. Training
3. Fellowship
4. Mission + Justice?
5. Koinonia / Intimacy groups
6. Legacy / Retirement

Preface

Before You Decide if This Book Is for You . . .

First of all, thank you for picking up a copy of this book, looking at its title, and deciding it's worth a minute of your time to turn some of the pages.

Each of these small acts says something significant about you. At the very least it means you're one of the curious who want to satisfy themselves as to what the book is about. It could also mean you're always on the lookout for a fresh approach to personal growth and loving relationships. It could even mean that you're ready to try for a major breakthrough into a more mature and probing, more sophisticated and satisfying philosophy of life.

If any of these expectations are true of you, please take another moment and read further.

Many other books along the shelf where you found this one also promise some insights into love, personal growth, and marriage. Most of them are excellent, written by authorities with years of experience. And most of them address questions that millions of people are asking about. If you study the titles of books on the subject, you will find that they fall into two main categories. A large number of current books on marriage promise the reader some help in maintaining the relationship, ensuring its

6

survival and continuity. You see phrases such as "making marriage last," "keeping love alive," "staying power," and the familiar "happily ever after" and "till death do us part." This says to me that a lot of couples seem to feel that what they have is pretty good, and they certainly don't want to lose it. Most of the books I see that address the desire to make a good marriage deliver what they promise. And the topic will continue to be popular far into the future.

The second type of book on marriage accounts for most of the rest that's written on the subject. The titles of these books are noticeable for their use of words that start with "re-": "recapturing the joy," "rekindling the pleasure," "rediscovering the magic." It's fair to say these titles imply that a lot of couples aren't as happy now as they used to be. They're looking for ways to go back to the good times. A book that can deliver on that promise will enjoy a wide circulation.

In the face of all these books from which you could choose, I confess that I'm a little nervous. Like the first group of authors, I'm deeply committed to strengthening and improving marriages that are already good. And like the second group, I believe it's always better to get back in touch with what's right in a relationship than to just allow it to keep on getting worse.

From my perspective, however, there is so much more to discover in a relationship that these other approaches never quite realize! It's my conviction that love and marriage are dynamic, growing, flowing processes. They start out with all the pleasures of new beginnings, and they also offer the possibility of getting better all the time. *I believe the best way to make a good marriage better is to keep it moving toward richer, more rewarding stages of maturity*—which is the natural right of human relationships. And I believe the best way to heal a hurting marriage, one that's lost its early glow, is to become more aware of the deeper levels of happiness that belong to you, which you may not have tapped, that are yours by virtue of the richness that is built into the very process of living. It's not hidden somewhere in the past; it's within the grasp of every one of us today.

If we're not careful, we will allow the "happily ever after" approach to lead us to view marriage as a marathon race, where lovers must learn to pace themselves, not expect too much too soon, and play it safe when it comes to trying new expressions or new dimensions of love.

Or, we will allow our relationship to become like a spinning top that starts out whirling and humming along, and then begins to run down until we must pump it every so often to get it going again.

But suppose love is, as I believe, an unfolding process. Then some other images are a lot more apt.

You might compare the growth of a marriage to that of a tree: Each year another ring of experience is added to the core. The original center is always there, so you don't need to "rediscover" it but to let it affect each successive ring in order to bring new power and possibility to the whole.

Here's another image that I like, even though it's rather prosaic. Love is like a timed-release capsule that you take for winter colds. Inside the capsule, all mingled together, are tiny pellets of healing, programmed to dissolve into your bloodstream at various time intervals—some in ten minutes, others in an hour, still others in three hours. When you enter a relationship, some of what you receive affects you immediately, in the experiences of initial attraction, falling in love, celebrating the honeymoon. (By the way, did you know? The word "honeymoon" originally referred to the way the autumn moon comes up over the horizon as a gigantic golden orb, which after a few moments shrinks to normal size as it moves higher in the sky. Not a very apt image for the view of marriage I want to explore in this book.) Like a timed-release capsule, love also releases new forms of energy when it's time to set up a living environment together, and when it's time to work at adjusting to each other's needs, habits, temperaments. Still other resources emerge at later stages to help deal creatively with the more sophisticated challenges of establishing and reassessing our deepest values and priorities. It's all there with us at the beginning, but we don't always have the wisdom to know where to look for it or to know how to use it.

Bear with me for a third image. Think of love as a kind of multi-stage rocket that has been the vehicle for sending people to the moon and for sending exploratory instruments beyond our solar system into the far reaches of our galaxy. How is love like a rocket? Well, both use up the most fuel overcoming gravity and getting launched. The launch is the most problematic stage for

8

both. Then they both go through a booster stage that allows for building to traveling speed and makes sure they're headed in the right direction. Finally, both enter the much longer, more friction-free stage, where the true mission can begin, where a journey of enlightenment propels them to the outer reaches of the experienced universe.

This book is about movement, motion, momentum; action, process, flow; journey, pilgrimage. And it's about experiencing these phenomena as part of a relationship as well as personally. You'll learn how a relationship partakes of group dynamics, since it is a group (albeit the smallest one). You'll see how you are affected by your relationship just as you are affected by being a part of any group (up to and including a stadium full of football fans), which influences you to act differently than if you were home watching the game on TV. Marriage is more subtle than that but no less powerful in what it does to you and for you.

This gives you some idea of the feel of this book. I'd just like to take another couple of minutes to say very succinctly what else you can expect to find here. I can do it best by unpacking the title for you.

The "Five Divorces." The momentum of marriage is sometimes interrupted. Periods of disequilibrium halt seasons of equilibrium. Then a new stage of harmony and balance sets in, better than anything you'd experienced before. Sometimes the interruptions are so serious that people think the relationship is at an end, especially when they're unaware of what's happening. And sometimes the relationship dies because no one knew how to deal with the transition. It may feel as though a divorce is on the way, when actually it is only one stage that is dying. In this sense, every "stage" ends in a "divorce." But the good news is that the new stage is better than the one you leave behind. And the even better news is that you don't even leave it behind for good. You leave it only until the new stage has settled in.

Of a Healthy Marriage. The impetus of this book is toward vitality and intimacy. The phrase "the five divorces" challenges the imagination with a new vision of love that can excite both the long-term married and the divorced. There is a common experience shared by all of us, whatever our marital state, a common experience that we can use to help each other through difficult times. But ultimately this book is a celebration of marriage. It is an expression of gratitude for my own experience of a loving partner in marriage. And it's an invitation to explore the possibilities of love that are out there ahead of all of us.

Marriage exists alongside a lot of other relationships, and they're all important: friendship, work associations, parenting, patronage of worthy causes, patriotism, eroticism, fraternity, sorority, serendipity (you continue the list). But they all depend on marriage as the most versatile and comprehensive of all the forms of human connectedness. They all select some traits and deemphasize others of the many levels of consciousness and the many aspects of community that we experience in marriage.

As goes marriage in our society, so goes all its derivative forms of interaction. To me as a professional communicator and as an amateur spouse, it's worth the closest attention I can give.

To Carole
in the beginning
of our twenty-fifth year

Introduction

How This Book Originated

I remember very well the time when a little voice inside told me I would have to write this book. It started in a quite unlikely place for a book on love. It was an academic setting—one of the ivoriest towers in the world, the five-hundred-year-old University of Tuebingen, nestled in the Swaebisch Alps of southwestern Germany. Intellectual? Campus streets were named after famous alumni: Melanchthon, Kant, Hegel, Holderlin. Outside the big lecture hall lay a rolling, wooded cemetery, the way you'd expect to see it outside a country church. Here were interred many professors of the famed nineteenth-century "Tuebingen School" of theology—pioneers of modern methods of textual research.

I had come to Germany with my wife and two children, in order to pursue a postgraduate research project. In its way, it was a project in communications: the new understanding of life and faith that was produced by the technological advance of printing Bibles for the masses. Carole and I were supporting ourselves by writing books and television scripts for a national broadcasting ministry based in Texas.

During our third and final year at Tuebingen, a guest professor from America arrived to lecture and lead a seminar on current trends in American thought. We had known the professor before, as I had taken several courses from him when I was a student at Harvard Divinity School. He was the theologian and historian Dr. Herbert W. Richardson, author of such books as *The Idea of an American Theology* and *Nun, Witch and Playmate: The Americanization of Sex.*

Students were expecting to hear about all the tumultuous developments in American thought of the sixties: the revolutionary ideologies and rhetoric, the human potential movements, the experiments with sex and drugs and new religions. Knowing Herb Richardson to be a spellbinding lecturer, in style almost a throwback to the old tent evangelists, I was eager to see how his content and style would be received in this citadel of German intellectual exactitude.

The first lecture was interesting enough, though cautious by my standard of a Herb Richardson lecture. It ended with the announcement that a discussion session would be held at a specified time and place.

We all assembled in a small room in which the chairs had been stacked in a corner and the students sat informally on tables set against the walls. When Professor Richardson entered, he smiled, greeted some quietly, but said nothing to the group. Soon five minutes had passed, then ten. We all looked to Dr. Richardson to start the discussion.

Instead—more silence, embarrassing, uncomfortable silence. We'd exchange quick glances, then look down. So unexpected was this kind of beginning that many of us felt intense anxiety, even pain. Suddenly one person, an American, burst out laughing. Soon she was in tears. She struggled to get control of her voice to say, "This silence is killing me. Doesn't anybody else feel the way I do?" And some other students reached out to comfort her. But for most of the time remaining, we sat in excruciating silence, occasionally interrupted by murmurings of one person to another. No one spoke up to lead the discussion. At last, without saying a word, the professor got up and left.

The next week, at the lecture hour, the hall was filled. People had heard about the seminar. Now Dr. Richardson began to speak. He explained that the seminar was an attempt to demonstrate a theory that was being tested in some American research centers: the theory that groups are not mere collections of individuals but that they express a kind of "corporate personality," which develops in much the same way as an individual personality. What we had experienced at the seminar, he said, was the conception, the fetal development, and the birth of a seminar group—the birth cry being the outburst of one of our members, uttered on behalf of us all. By remaining silent, and experiencing the birth of the group personality as a shared experience, we had seen it from the inside far more demonstrably and dramatically than if we'd only heard a professor lecture about it.

Then Dr. Richardson made some predictions about what would happen in the next seminar and the ones following. He said that we would first concern ourselves with structuring the meetings so that we would not lapse into silence again. He also spoke of later attempts to establish leadership and to focus on coursework goals, grading methods, and ways to see that decisions were arrived at and enforced fairly. He said that our knowing in advance what was to happen wouldn't influence events much because events followed a certain sequence that recapitulated aspects of our own personality development.

In later weeks of lectures, we heard that our group would ultimately reach a stage like that of adolescence, in which our conflicting group goals and values would break out into the open. For we were a group that included Germans, Americans, and other nationalities; Protestants and Catholics; liberals and conservatives; Marxists and apoliticals. He also predicted that at some point our conflicts would lead us to declare independence from an authority figure—as a way of uniting ourselves in a common goal so that we could get past our conflicts. We would, he said, decide to expel the professor from the class.

I won't describe all the meetings, the jockeying among individuals for authority to speak for the various groups, and the floating coalitions that formed as the various groups struggled to impose some order. But I will never forget the electrifying day when we did actually banish Dr. Richardson from the class. Nor will I ever forget his parting words—that this was a very real event, that he was not coming back, that he was returning to America, and that it was up to us to decide how our participation would be graded, and how we would describe what had happened when the dean of the theological faculty asked for an explanation.

It was then that I began creating a theoretical model of human behavior that would account for the strange symmetry in our group experience. Could it be true that groups have a collective personality? Could groups actually recapitulate the stages of growth of the individual personality? And what about Dr. Richardson's other assertion, that both individual and group development recapitulate the stages of human cultural development throughout history—could that be true? And I began to wonder how anyone could prove such a theory.

I believed that I had experienced the development of a group consciousness in the class that semester. And what I knew of personality development seemed to correspond in very significant ways. Since I had spent most of my adult life in the study and practice of interpersonal communications, I felt I was onto something important that very few people were aware of as they charted the ups and downs of adult life and relationships.

It was then that a little voice inside me began to say that I should not let this experience go, that I should keep digging into the subject of group dynamics and personality development, adding them to my years of study in the history of ideas and the history of culture, just to see if it makes sense to say there is a pattern here, or whether it's all random and unpredictable and not terribly relevant to our understanding of what human development is all about.

And so for the last decade and a half I have carried on an avocation of reading, attending seminars, and interviewing experts who seemed to have something to say about my interests. I became aware of the new disciplines of cognitive development, led by the Swiss psychologist Jean Piaget, and of moral development, pioneered by Harvard researcher Lawrence Kohlberg. I especially have received much from my reading and personal contacts with James W. Fowler of Emory University, who has outlined the stages of moral and ethical development in adulthood. I also followed the debates over the work of Erik Erikson, Daniel J. Levinson, and others, as popularized in Gail Sheehy's books *Passages* and *Pathfinders*, in which the biological and physiological changes in adult life are shown to affect the way we approach our values.

But the most significant impact of all has been the incomparable value of having a partner with whom to compare my experiences. My wife, Carole, is a true co-author of this book. She is the one with training in developmental psychology. And she is the one with years of experience in working with preschool children on a professional basis, employing the insights about cognition and readiness in her own work and in our family life.

She is also the person who made it easy to focus my thoughts and theories on the most basic of all interpersonal relationships, the intimacy and love in marriage. It was only about five years ago that I realized that marriage is, among all the other things it is, a true testing ground for focusing insights about group dynamics, interpersonal communication, and cultural development. It is also a most rewarding and enjoyable part of life, one that is most open to new ideas.

So with Carole as a great partner in the conversation, I have developed the ideas that will unfold in the chapters that follow. This book will describe how love is a process of growth:

—That a relationship develops a life of its own, and that every relationship has its own personality, just as we speak of a corporate personality or a national or cultural identity.

—That love grows according to certain predictable and almost universal sequences of our childhood personality development, and can be expected to unfold in the same order for most people, being grounded in the growth sequence of infancy, childhood, preadolescence, adolescence, and postadolescence.

—That the growth of love is based on cognitive and moral discoveries as much if not more than the natural external changes based on aging. (Otherwise, why do people vary so widely in their responses to marriage, having children, building careers, facing an empty nest, beginning retirement, and the like? I believe that our perspectives affect our experiences at least as much as our experiences affect our perspectives.)

—That the growth of love, being cognitive and moral, goes through periods of disequilibrium that are necessary parts of the process of breakthrough and assimilation inherent in all change for the better.

These are some of the basics that I will be exploring. This is just the beginning, a preliminary inquiry. You're invited to participate, to compare your own experiences, to challenge the parts that don't match your own experience, and to use the parts that make you aware of your experience so that the full possibilities of love can come alive for you.

The Stages of Love: Some Definitions

As in most works that venture into areas where not many others have gone, this book has had to invent some words and to use some existing words in somewhat new ways. The words for the stages of love presented that kind of a problem. It is common today to lament the ways we use the word *love* so carelessly that the hearer has to translate it immediately, depending on the context, as momentary attraction, or dynamic commitment, or romantic fascination, or sacrificial compassion. C. S. Lewis' book *The Four Loves* selects four different ancient Greek words for love, which he uses to describe different modern experiences of loving. I have borrowed all four of these, using them in the way Lewis did, and have added two more Greek words to point to still other experiences or stages of love.

The Greek words that are used to define the stages of love are these:

Stage One: *Eros.* The earliest form of love between two people is modeled after love between mother and infant. It is marked by feelings of incompleteness and dependency that can be assuaged only by physical closeness. For most adults, the *eros* stage is expressed in mutual attraction and the desire to be together. In the less mature relationships, however, such as those involving young teenagers trying to escape intolerable situations at home, both partners are looking for someone to nurture them, to complete the parenting process. In the more mature relationships, *eros* is the mutual expression of physical, emotional, intellectual, and spiritual intimacy. In all relationships based on *eros*, however, the issue soon arises of how to maintain continuity, how to build a daily existence together. For some, daily routine seems to be the enemy of *eros*, and a crisis arises that forces a choice between the two. For others, the need to face the issue of daily routine produces the opportunity to move into the next stage.

Stage Two: *Storge.* This is the Greek word for affection, domestic love, the enjoyment of doing simple things together. It is the period of deciding who will handle the finances, who will make the repairs, and who will care for the lawn. It is the stage when roles and rules are established, and when marriage partners try to blend the customs and habits of their parents in a way that satisfies them. Some couples have difficulty making conscious decisions about these routines and get locked into rigid rules and

17

roles. Others see marriage as a continuing process in which the roles and rules must be redefined through the years. The challenge to transcend *storge* provides the second "divorce."

Stage Three: *Philia.* This is the Greek word for friendship. Friendship marriage is love based on common values rather than common activities, roles, and rules. It is the stage when couples enjoy sharing their feelings, fears, and fantasies with each other. For a man and a woman to be able to share on this level of intimacy, they must learn to transcend the gender gap. Some individuals feel comfortable confiding their intimate thoughts only to someone of the same sex. They are more likely to talk over their marital problems, if they talk at all, with a fellow member of the bowling team or one of the "girls" in the carpool. For these, a marriage based on friendship remains a distant goal, attainable only as they delve into the origins of their preference for same-sex intimacy. Other couples, however, eventually find Stage Three too conventional, comfortable, confining. Their sense of adventure, discovery, and freedom leads them to experiment with the possibilities of a new stage.

Stage Four: *Dikaiosune.* This is the Greek word for fairness, justice, equality. Many couples find this to be the ideal stage because here they can encourage each other to the maximum of personal growth, based on equality in the relationship. For others, however, this can be a painful and destructive time when, in the name of liberation, alternate lifestyles, and individualism, partners act out infantile self-deceptions and manipulations of others. As popular as this stage is as an ideal in our culture, it too is only part of a process. Some choose to go back to the security of friendship marriage; some find themselves caught in a loop of personal discoveries that prove alienating over the long term; and others feel a call to transcend the endless variations of experimentation and manipulation in order to find a depth of love that can hold longer than this year's self-discovery fad.

Stage Five: *Agape.* This is the Greek word for unconditional love. Breathes there a love that can flourish in the midst of change, survive tragedy and failure, and express itself authentically in a world of contradiction, paradox, absurdity? Is there a love that is stronger than death? Those who have experienced the Stage Five expression of love would answer yes. And nothing short of unconditional love can help us keep faith with each other, our commitments, responsibilities, social consciences, and deepest needs. Only *agape* could enable a couple to stay together for a lifetime when one partner is partially disabled, and the other partner must be the caregiver without retreating into the parent-child relationship. Only *agape* could enable a couple to reverse roles several times during a lifetime without feeling that either was retreating. Only *agape* could enable a couple to draw the complete benefits of all the earlier stages of love and not feel that they were somehow superior to persons struggling with the earlier stages. *Agape* is based on the sense of infinite mystery represented by another individual, mystery beyond knowledge, familiarity, or experience of another.

Stage Six: *Ktisis*. This is the Greek word for the creative act. Stage Six love is not described by its content but by its effect. It is a concept reserved for those few historic breakthroughs through the centuries in which a new stage of loving has emerged. This stage serves to remind us that all the forms of love, including the ones we take for granted, at one time were new upon the earth and met with great resistance as they appeared and spread throughout the culture. Most of those who made the most important contributions to the history of love are anonymous individuals, probably not consciously attempting to make history. The same is true of the individuals who today are making it possible for future generations to explore more deeply the infinite mystery of love.

	Styles of Loving	**Personality Stages**
I.	*Form* (handwritten) *Eros* desire longing	Infancy: —sense of wonder —dependency —learning basic trust
First Divorce	*Storm* (handwritten)	
II.	*Storge* affection domesticity love of the familiar	Childhood: —telling stories —learning rules —imitating adult behavior
Second Divorce	*Norm* (handwritten)	
III.	*Philia* friendship	Preadolescence: —replace rules with principles —role models —sexual latency
Third Divorce	*perform* (handwritten)	
IV.	*Dikaiosune* fairness justice rightness	Adolescence: —experimentation —self-discovery —independence
Fourth Divorce		
V.	*Agape* releasing liberating unconditional love	Postadolescence: —sympathy —living with tensions and paradoxes —acceptance of earlier stages
Fifth Divorce		
VI.		**New Pioneering: Beyond Today's**

A HEALTHY MARRIAGE

Cultural Influences

Characteristics of Love Relationships

Primitive Tribes:
(Before 3000 B.C.)
—human survival
—impersonal tribal identity
—love as sacrifice

—deep-seated needs met
—falling of barriers
—desire for continuation

Early Civilizations:
(3000-1000 B.C.)
—villages, laws, patriarchs,
   armies
—rewards for good
—punishment for evil

—live under same roof
—accept traditional
   roles
—adjust to differences

World Civilizations:
(1000 B.C.-A.D. 1500)
—brotherhood of humanity
—spiritual equality
—universal truth to all

—share common values
—build family ties
—serve in community

Rise of Science, Exploration,
Democracy (1500-1900):
—control over natural
   world
—struggle for world
   domination
—clash of cultures

—mutual encouragement
   to grow
—personal change not
   threatening
—unconventional lifestyles
   not divisive

Space Age (20th century):
—coexistence in
   pluralistic world
—environmental protection
—possibility for nuclear
   war and for life on
   other planets

—accept each other's
   vulnerability
—nonmanipulative
   communication
—knowledge and mystery
   increases

Personality and Cultural Developments

Stage One: *Eros*, Love as Dependency
The Infancy Period of a Relationship

Sex can be defined
fairly adequately in physiological terms
as consisting of the building up
of bodily tensions and their release.
Eros, in contrast, is the experiencing
of the personal intentions and meaning
of the act.
      —Rollo May, *Love and Will*[1]

Erotic love . . . is also perhaps the most
deceptive form of love there is. . . . it is often
confused with the experience of "falling"
in love, the sudden collapse of the barriers
that existed until that moment. . . . The "loved"
person becomes as well known as oneself.
Or, perhaps I should better say as little known.
      —Erich Fromm, *The Art of Loving*[2]

Do you remember how you first fell in love? If you're like most of us, you have stored away in your mind a narrative that you have created. It tells how the two of you first met, your initial feelings for each other, which of you was the first to recognize that a serious relationship was developing, and how the events fell into place leading up to your decision to marry.

22

Even though every couple's story is different (and even though the same story may survive the years in different versions), certain basic events seem to be common to every relationship that develops into a marriage.

Falling in Love: Some Common Experiences

First impressions. One fascinating way to deepen our understanding of a relationship is to compare memories of first impressions. How do we feel about the possibility of "love at first sight"? Some people have more vivid memories of their first impressions than others, yet we all do experience them, whether we take them seriously or not. Most of us know both long-lasting and short-lived relationships that were said to be love at first sight, just as we know of both long and short relationships that needed a long runway to take off.

The classic experiences of love at first sight, endlessly recaptured in song and story, follow certain patterns familiar to all of us:

Two people meet. They begin to sense that this is different, that "I already know this person." I understand what this person is saying and feeling. I am drawn closer and closer. Barriers are falling, one after another. We know each other at more and more levels. We like what we see, and are drawn farther and farther into each other's lives. There is a sense that events are beyond our control, that we are falling, like free-fall parachutists, unafraid of falling, for in some way we are in ultimate control of what is happening. Perhaps that is why generations still call it "falling" in love.

Most relationships, long or short, experience this sense of falling barriers. It doesn't seem to matter whether it happened immediately, at "first sight," or whether it took longer to develop. It is this lack of resistance that propels us into a deepening relationship. When we meet resistance, and run into barriers in knowing each other, our progress is slowed. It becomes harder to cross new frontiers together. The relationship begins to stall.

In some circumstances, two people in an amazingly short time can pass through barrier after barrier without experiencing much resistance at all. There is infatuation, yes, attraction on a physical level. But there is more. And it is immediately present.

23

So to be technical about it, we can plot falling in love on a grid, a quadrant. Imagine a horizontal line that plots the rate of speed from faster to slower. And picture a vertical line that plots the degree of depth of the relationship from short-lived to long-lived. We all know of relationships that fit into each quadrant: (1) fast-starting, short-lived; (2) fast-starting, long-lived; (3) slow-starting, short-lived; and (4) slow-starting, long-lived.

It's interesting for couples to compare their impressions as to which quadrant best describes their relationship. Sometimes the two agree, sometimes not. There's probably a good reason for this. It may be an example of the contention that a relationship is like a first child—partly coming from each partner, and partly developing a life of its own. From the very beginning, a relationship is different from either partner's perception of it. That's why it can be so revealing to go back at various times and re-examine our memories of the early days.

In beginning such a review, it often becomes quickly apparent that people differ in what they remember. A couple's "love story" varies depending on who is telling it. And the story often changes over the years. Perspectives change. Memories become more selective. Current issues get in the way. So retelling the love story through the years is a healthy way to notice subtle and slow shifts in the tone of a relationship. Going over the early details may reveal the origins of certain expectations, disappointments, and personal needs that have continued to exert a great influence on the marriage without anyone's knowing it.

Take for example the question of "who first realized it was love." Partners may differ about the time, place, and even the person who made the discovery. What accounts for the differences? It may not be the facts that matter. The real difference may lie in two people's attitudes toward "love at first sight." One partner might be more trustful of intuitive judgments. The other might put more confidence in a gradual, cumulative approach to decision making. Their differing interpretations of what is happening might lead the outside observer to conclude that these two aren't even talking about the same relationship! In some ways that would be true. One might be more impressed with the early part of the process of meeting, seeing the ongoing relationship as an extension of the "first sight," while the other might be more aware of the process that led to the end result. These attitudes

24

toward intuition and trust in gradual processes commonly are formed very early in life.

The relationship itself is a product of both first impressions and gradual processes. It continues to develop in ways that are unknown to the two partners. It's as if there are three perspectives that need to be taken into account: his, hers, and the relationship's.

Still, there is something to the point that relationships differ in terms of both the rate of speed at which they develop and the depth at which people come to know each other.

Erich Fromm makes a point about a fast-developing relationship in which the lovers come to know each other as well as they know themselves—"or as poorly." Here is an example of the fast-starting, short-lived affair. Intuition fails the couple in this case; they confuse intensity with authenticity. Ultimately, our capacity for intimacy depends on our capacity for self-knowledge.

Statistics bear this out. The highest rate of divorce today comes from marriages among teenagers, especially among school dropouts. The ability to make critical judgments quickly comes with experience. We realize that one mark of immaturity is overestimating one's ability to cope with difficult situations. It may not be that immature persons base their judgments too much on physical attraction; it may be that their ability to judge all levels of interaction—emotional, intellectual, and spiritual as well—is less developed.

There are people whose relationship is of the fast-starting, long-lasting variety. Most of us know a couple who were engaged and married after a whirlwind courtship and who have built a strong marriage. What accounts for the difference? It may be a more highly developed ability to know oneself and to look deeply into the life of another person.

We know from current research on perception and cognition that the human mind works with amazing, computer-like speed to process information. Often we are not even conscious of the process by which we determine whether an encounter with another person bodes danger, friendliness, or even love. The brain seems to be able to process a great deal of experience in about the same time it takes to process a small amount. So the person with more experience is at an advantage in trusting intuition. A highly trained emergency worker can move decisively, quickly, and effectively in a chaotic situation because the mind can send instructions as fast as the body can respond to them. A less experienced person gets a variety of confusing signals to flee, fight, improvise, or be cautious, all of which tend to cancel out each other.

This sounds like the plight of the person who keeps getting involved in slow-starting, short-lived relationships. The attraction is there, but the message is muddled. Other signals keep interfering, such as: Who can you trust anyway? What is love? Am I up to this? What if this person really knew me? It's hard to launch a relationship when the runway is strewn with obstacles.

The slow-starting but long-lasting marriages seem to be the safest of all, but not for the obvious reasons. Caution is not always a virtue. Slow drivers can be the most dangerous on the road. And durability has its down side, in predictability and sameness. What the slow-starters but long-lasters do have going for them may well be something else: the capacity to get the most out of their experience. Unlike the fast-starters, they are more sensitive to the cumulative effect of their experiences. They might feel that you don't glimpse all the future in one blinding flash; rather, you get lots of glimpses and lots of flashes, and each one has its own unique effect on those that came before and those that come after. Then, unlike the short-livers, this group learns to make sense out of the conflicting information that is a part of every life. Instead of being immobilized and defeated by it, long-livers integrate it, see patterns in it, find uses for it.

The purpose of this book is twofold: to hold out hope that all of us can use the conflicts in our relationships to create new levels of intimacy; and to help us all make use of our intuition, our experience, our decision-making abilities, our capacities for intimacy.

Just because a couple were married as teenage dropouts doesn't mean they're destined for the statistical dead end. Only a couple of generations ago, marriages of teenagers who didn't graduate from high school were the norm in America. Such marriages still are customary in many parts of the world; and the divorce rates are often much lower than they are here. One thing is clear: Something has attacked this traditional mode of marriage in recent years and inflicted a higher death rate than among those who deferred marriage for more education, career experience, and emotional maturity.

26

That brings up the element of historical perspective. Every era and every culture seems to create a form of marriage that it can encourage, reinforce, and multiply. It may be that a new style of marriage is now emerging that is more appropriate to our own time than traditional forms. If the result is that love is more of a process than an institution, we should not be surprised by the changes. It would be naive, though, to look down on the pain and tragedy of broken relationships from some lofty perspective and view them as mere growing pains for a new society. Most of the evil committed in the world was said to be justified in the name of a higher purpose. It is necessary to keep both a sense of history and a close attention to our own personal experiences. One good way to keep both values is to create a historical perspective of our own lives, our own development as persons—and then to build on that foundation a sense of the process that our marriage followed.

That's why we can use the metaphors of infancy, childhood, and adolescence and apply them to love. These concepts of growth and development can suggest some powerful ideas for making sense of the chaos and creativity of relationships today.

Infancy: The First Experiences of Love

The period of infancy introduces us to experiences of love that stay with us as long as we live. Our infancy is like the innermost ring of a tree—formed in the first year and remaining at the center as the other rings are added year by year. Our early experiences of loving set the tone for our personality development, our capacity for relating to others. And then, later, when we begin a journey with another person, we can see parallels between that relationship's infancy period and each partner's earliest experiences. The closer we look at love in infancy, the more we are led to wonder if our relationship might not actually imitate or recapitulate the infancy experiences of the two partners.

Some areas where the parallels are most intriguing are: dependency, trust, wonder, bonding, naive realism, giving.

Dependency: Love as the Gift of Life Itself

Love comes to us long before we are born, down a one-way street, through countless generations. We are totally dependent on this biological heritage for our very existence. The first way

27

love comes to us is as the gift of life itself. From the standpoint of biology, our first appearance in life is as a molecular combination of our fathers and mothers. We are nothing in and of ourselves. Even long after we are born our genetic dependency continues. We inherit certain traits in the way we look and behave. Our physical appearance borrows various features—hair and eye color, nose and lip configurations, disease immunity or susceptibility—from our parents and our family line. We never completely escape our biological dependency; we simply continue to add other stages of growth to it.

No more elemental act of love exists than the gift of life itself. When as an infant I receive the gift of life, I accept it with no effort or merit or obligation on my part. I participate in the first of many acts of love in which my response is simply to accept the gift and to share in it.

It is not always easy to accept this gift of life so freely and then to pass it on freely to others. Some of us take on a sense of obligation and duty as we grow up. A gift may become a sign that we owe someone a debt instead of a reminder that life itself is ultimately a gift. In some cases the feeling of dependency exerts such a strong influence that a gift triggers suspicion and resentment, reminders of a person's weakness over against the world. For most people most of the time, though, a gift inspires feelings of surprise, delight, and joy, a mutual bond of appreciation, sharing, remembrance.

So when an attractive person appears in our midst, that encounter is also a gift. Our response to that person flows from all our experiences of receiving gifts. Suspicion and indebtedness, or joy and delight—this is what we bring to the encounter from memories of our very earliest moments of life. Our varying responses have much to do with our deepest feelings about dependency. And those feelings go back to our earliest moves toward independence, which were fueled by the development of basic trust.

Basic Trust: The Source of Growth Toward Independence

As unborn children all of us had both a biological and a psychological dependency on the womb. When we were suddenly pulled out of that environment, we were ushered into a larger womb whose boundaries were as wide as the universe. We moved from being totally surrounded by our mothers to living side by side with them. We moved from being passively nourished by natural sources of oxygen and food to having to breathe for ourselves and work for our food. We still had physical dependencies on food and rest. And we still had emotional needs to be held as securely and warmly as we were back in the womb.

As the days went by, though, an amazing natural process began to unfold. We started becoming a little less physically dependent on our mothers.

In one important sign of progress, we began to accept the sight of our mothers as an acceptable substitute for their immediate physical presence. The sight of Mother helped us to be reassured that all the rest of her powers we depended on were still there.

As more time passed, we began to accept sound as a substitute for sight. We could feel secure in simply hearing Mother bustling around in another room, singing or talking. Those familiar sounds became a new, more abstract kind of reassurance. It's as though each of us somehow figured, "Even if I can't see Mother, I can hear her. That voice reminds me that all the other things I depend on are still there. So I don't have to cling to the physical body of my mother all the time in order to be assured that my needs will be met and that I'll stay alive."

Later on there came a time when we discovered that our shouts and cries could change Mother's behavior. As if by magic, we could change the invisible voice of Mother from the other room into the visible presence of Mother near us. That sense of power gave us the reassurance that comes from being able to interact with the environment. Formerly helpless infants, you and I began to have that first sense of being able to control a situation. When that happened, the dependency equation between infant and mother began to change.

As infants we would remain dependent for a long time, but no longer would we be helpless. In fact, there soon came a point when Mother's actual presence was no longer needed; our memory picture was enough.

In these earliest days of life, love manifested itself to us as protection of the weaker by the stronger. It was still a one-way relationship, but it was changing. The effectiveness of our moves toward independence had a lot to do with the consistency with

29

which our parents offered their care. Erratic behavior on their part may have prolonged our dependency needs. And neglectful behavior by our parents may have permanently affected our approach to later relationships.

Here is an example: Every parent faced the dilemma of what to do when the baby cried. Some parents were taught that they should let their infant cry, that picking it up would "spoil" it. Others believed they should treat it like the telephone—always pick it up as soon as it rings. In reality, neither method has the support of all the experts. But consistent reactions probably speeded our ability to affect our environment. Crying in order to be picked up was an early way we learned to break the hold of total dependency, and the sooner we found something that worked, whatever it was, the better.

As we continued to become physically less dependent, we learned how to combine all the sounds and sights, the touches and memories, of our earliest life. We traded one physical dependency after another for a different kind: an emotional dependency. There followed other physical developments toward independence, as we learned to talk, to walk, to move through the world, to move the world.

Today as adults, our memories resonate with these early experiences with dependency in our love relationships. If our infancy needs were neglected by our parents to the point of abusive treatment, some of us may well be carrying scars that can be healed only with therapy and counseling. Some of us may have grown up to be adults who lack a sense of self-worth, of confidence in our ability to make an impact as we would like. These persons may be doubting their right to live happily in the world. This lack of confidence may express itself in clumsy or even violent ways to make our presence felt. Whether passive or aggressive or both, we may remain fearful or suspicious about the value of any close relationships, especially those that render us vulnerable to another person.

If our infancy needs were met only spasmodically and inconsistently, we may have grown up feeling uncertain about what works and what doesn't in relating to other people. Self-doubt is often the result of an infancy in which we received contradictory signals about our parents' care. Maybe some of the time our cries were answered with responses to our needs, and part of the time

30

the cries brought on spankings. We would be faced with a terrible choice: the loneliness that came if we didn't cry for help, and a dreadful uncertainty—would it be pleasure or pain?—if we did cry. Anything is better, at times, than the terror of utter loneliness. And so we took the risk. As adults we may respond to loneliness the same way—seeking attention any way we can get it, including counter-productive and even self-destructive behavior.

If, on the other hand, our infancy needs were met with responsiveness and reassurance on the part of our parents, a good foundation has been laid. Basic trust is more likely to flourish. Responsiveness does not mean smothering, however. It means helping us get launched on the journey from dependency to independence. It means helping us move through the stages of physical and emotional dependence as naturally and smoothly as possible. Then as adults we view dependence and independence as parts of a continuity, not as conflicting values. We are better prepared to share our lives with others in mutual loving.

Wonder: The First Experience of the World

By the time we were two or three years old, we were seeing ourselves as part of a world full of novelty and wonder. Our bed, our room, our house, our yard, our neighborhood proved to be inexhaustible sources of enchantment and excitement. As young children, we saw every event as a new event. Everything that happened was a miracle, without cause or connection to other events.

As small children we didn't yet know any of the rules as to how things are supposed to work. We perceived events as a running series of episodes. Our minds tended to focus on one thing at a time. We couldn't use past experiences to build up predictable patterns. We couldn't yet reason that "if this happened yesterday then I can expect it to happen today." Each moment was a creation in itself. The present moment—unpredictable, uncontrollable—was our reality.

As adults we never completely lose this sense of wonder and magic, nor should we. It's always there for us, waiting to ignite a moment. Each encounter with another human being offers the potential of being swept into a new reality. Each time we stop to get in touch with our own thoughts and feelings promises us new discoveries about ourselves.

Yet this sense of magic and unpredictability can be either frightening or thrilling, depending on our experience of the world in our early years. If all through life we have run into one unpredictable situation after another, and if each new situation makes us feel helpless, exploited, or victimized, then the new in life will fill us with dread. But if our sense of wonder and magic has been allowed to blend with our sense of control and stability, then we can face the future eagerly and welcome our growth in love.

It is normal in very early childhood to experience the world as fluid and unpredictable, with the controls all outside our grasp. But it is tragic for an adult to do so, even when that adult may go through life filled with a childlike sense of wonder. For adults, playfulness and imagination are liberating when they are freely chosen, but imprisoning when we are given no choice.

Bonding: The First Experience of Relationship

Back in our infancy world, where anything could happen, each of us interacted with others simply by participating. We just played along. We still lacked a highly developed sense of how to interact with people. Even though we could cry and produce results, it took time for us to know our own strength.

We may have been adorably cute babies. Our smiles made people want to pick us up, hug us, and take care of us. At first this all happened naturally, as though some part of the genetic code had compensated for our helplessness by making us so compelling that the rest of the human race would welcome us. Later, however, we lost our innocence as we learned how to turn the charm on and off at will. A new power was in our hands, to use for or against ourselves, for or against others.

On our parents' side there was the matter of "bonding," the emotional and spiritual attachment of mothers, in particular, for their newborn infants. It generally occurs through close contact in the first few days of life. Sometimes bonding fails to occur due to isolation of infant from mother because of illness, depression, or anxiety. Responsiveness suffers. Infants and parents have to work harder to interact positively. Recent research in child abuse and neglect points to factors in both the infant's personality and the parent's that set up barriers to bonding. Sometimes the result is that children have to resort to increasingly desperate measures to get attention. Sometimes it gets to the point of risking punishment (literally "asking for it") as preferable to no attention at all. "Asking for it" may carry over into adulthood, where it affects our love relationships. We are after intensity of feeling first and foremost; whether the feelings are pleasurable or painful is secondary.

Naive Realism: The First Philosophy of Life

Another assumption you and I made as small children was that all people experience things the same way we do. We could walk up to a stranger on the street and announce, "Johnny got a new bike." We didn't realize some people didn't know Johnny. Our naiveté enabled us to do a lot of cute things like smiling and waving at strangers in the store, meeting the new neighbors before our parents did, repeating things we heard our parents say. It provided a lot of entertainment for the family, but it also provided an important transitional step toward interacting with others. We were on the way to discovering the concept of individuality. Our perceptions were new to us. We didn't ask if they were new to anyone else.

It's easy to admire this childlike innocence, this easy trust of strangers. Sometimes we envy the charm, the accepting way of interacting. And as a dimension of a mature relationship it's something we never need to outgrow. It can be destructive, however, if we never develop powers of discrimination between what is safe and what is dangerous, if we never accept the responsibilities of making critical decisions, if we never learn to separate our own point of view from the views of others.

Philosophers call this view of life "naive realism." According to this view, things are pretty much what they appear to be. And everyone sees things the same way we do. A red ball looks red to us because its redness is out there, around the ball. All my eyes do is see it.

In relationships, naive realism refers to the assumption that there is only one way to feel about any particular situation. It comes out in thoughts like these:

"If a situation made me angry, then that's how you should feel too."

"If you don't feel the way I feel, you're just being stubborn."

"Don't bother to explain. I know all I need to know."

"You know you're wrong; you just won't admit it."

"I told you so."

These are expressions of an arrested development of perspective. They fail to make the leap into another person's experience, to see events from more than one point of view. Most people, most of the time, have the capacity to get beyond naive realism. (Whether we always live up to our potential is another question.) We were given this capacity along with the arrival of a strong sense of self. Security as a unique person had to come first. Once we had developed confidence in our own ability to perceive reality, we could begin the process of letting others do the same. We no longer needed uniformity of thought from others to reassure us of our own frail sense of personhood.

Naive realism is a necessary step in the process of learning to interact with another person. Those who never developed a strong sense of self may spend years of adulthood trying to establish it. One of the first signs of victory is the capacity to hold to your own point of view while understanding the perspective of another person.

Giving: Love Experienced as Sacrifice

Once a child has developed a strong sense of trust and independence, the capacity to love also begins to change. No more is the child the passive recipient of a parent's love. A child learns to give as well as receive. Again the key is the development of a healthy sense of self. When a child can feel distinct from all the surrounding sights, sounds, experiences, and people, the earlier world that was fluid, magic, and unpredictable begins to look different.

Giving and receiving love becomes possible for us even in our infancy and early childhood. But we must know where to look for the signs. We don't start out knowing how to offer great acts of generosity. Our spontaneous giving of joy through our smiles, gurgles, and hugs are at first natural gifts of grace which we do not control. Later, we learn to control them to our own advantage, as part of our development of strong personalities, and then we are prepared to become giving human beings. No one can give what she or he does not have. That may be why so many people enter adulthood still looking for ways to find relationships where mutual sharing is possible.

When a small child's ego is still in the formation process, giving or sharing can appear as loss, as sacrifice. It can cause fear,

34

grief, and pain. Being asked to give away one stick of candy, to share a toy, to help a parent, are acts of loving that come from a strongly defined sense of self.

We've all watched a child walking across the room holding armfuls of bulky toys, barely managing them all. But if we offer to help by carrying one of the toys, we're apt to get a noisy protest. The child can't see our motive. It looks like we're trying to take something away.

For some adults, love is still a finite commodity in short supply, particularly to them. Love must be measured out slowly, so as not to lose too much. You've got to watch out for the people who are trying to take away your love, as these adults see it, or else you'll be victimized again.

Our struggle with feelings like these reminds us that we're still involved in developing a strong and healthy self-image. The fluid, unpredictable world out there still can threaten to sweep over us, take our personhood away. The real drama in life is not about sharing love, but about siding with the forces of order against the forces of chaos; between the multitudes and the individual. Under these circumstances, lasting love is rarely possible. At best, two weak egos in search of personhood may find each other and recognize their common struggle. But it will be hard for them to share the search, since sharing stems from a different set of assumptions about the world. Instead, they may simply reinforce each other's fears, suspicions, and hurts. Each fuels the other's sense of love as loss and sacrifice.

Sometimes a person with a weak sense of self becomes involved with someone who appears to have a strong ego. Even here, the unevenness of the relationship too often leads to trouble. The "strong" partner may be a weak person trying to build strength by taking on the role of a parent. Such a person may be sending parent messages to others, which are interpreted incorrectly as strength by people who haven't learned to tell the difference. And so the two people engage in trying to grow up by acting out parent-child games all their lives. Neither partner has moved out of a Stage One level of relating.

It is tempting to go a step further and speculate about the views of love held by those who view themselves as great lovers and benefactors of others. The newspapers are full of stories about men called "womanizers" who spread their love generously and prodigally among as many partners as possible. And there are other stories about people who give money away in extravagant amounts, many times to valid worthy causes. Not all persons who act generously toward humanity in general are struggling with a degree of arrested development, of course. The chapter on Stage Five looks more carefully at *agape* forms of love. Still, one wonders whether some of the more spectacular episodes are not attempts to buy love, respect, and admiration from the multitudes, while failing to develop the same capacities in one-on-one relationships.

We must leave our thoughts about infantile expressions of loving. It is time to take a closer look at the ways that our earliest experiences influence the early stages of our relationships, to tie together the two principal sections of this chapter so far.

Three Couples in the Infancy Stage of Marriage

Our infancies surely influence us in a variety of ways. And when it comes to love, our infancies seem to exert a special influence on the early years of marriage, when our relationship itself is in its infancy. One good way to explore these influences is to imagine how they might affect the lives of actual couples engaged in the real-life struggles and adventures of loving. So this is a good time to introduce three couples who will be with us as we cross all the thresholds, experience all the "five divorces" of a healthy marriage.

Here are Allen and Barbara, Charlie and Donna, Eddie and Fran. They are as real as people we know because they are composites of people we know. Novelists often create their characters out of traits and experiences of their own friends and acquaintances. Behavioral scientists find that the use of composite characters, or "typologies," helps focus on the important aspects of their studies.

Our three couples will be introduced as they first met and married, in the infancy stage of their relationships.

Allen and Barbara

Allen was a talented artist and Barbara was a political activist when they met in University City. They quickly perceived each other's abilities even though they were not well versed in each other's strengths. Very quickly they came to know a great deal about each other. Time flew when they were together. When they were apart, working in their chosen fields, they missed each other but felt strangely that what they were doing would be the subject of spirited conversations when they got together.

Early in the relationship marriage became a real option. The longer they knew each other, the more they felt they were right for each other. Allen and Barbara were married in a big family ceremony that simply made public what they had felt for each other almost from the beginning.

Charlie and Donna

Donna met Charlie in Friendsdale at a restaurant where she was working to pay for her freshman year in college. Charlie had recently graduated from a big university in another state and was working for a small, aggressive insurance company that had recently transferred him to Donna's hometown of Friendsdale.

When they went out, Charlie made Donna feel good that a young guy "out to make it" in business would give her so much attention. Even though this was her hometown, Charlie knew of interesting places to go that she had never seen before.

Donna helped Charlie feel at home in the new town. Her parents had lived there for years, and they took an instant liking to Charlie. This didn't hurt his ability to make contacts around town.

When Charlie and Donna got married, they settled down in Friendsdale in a nice old house nestled in a neighborhood with lots of kids—a house Donna's parents helped pay for.

Eddie and Fran

When Eddie first spotted Fran, she was dancing with the guy who had brought her to the nightclub. But Fran went home that night with Eddie. That showed Eddie what kind of impression he'd made on her. And he knew how she'd affected him. This time it was for real; Eddie and Fran both knew it. And they both were determined to avoid the mistakes they'd made with past relationships.

Eddie had been married before when he was nineteen. He divorced two years later. Fran was engaged once, to a guy who could be great at times but had a terrific temper. When that temper ignited with a little alcohol, there could be torrents of abusive words, threats, suspicions, even violence. And then the next day there was contrition, pleas for forgiveness, promises of change, and reminders of how good it was when it was good.

Eddie and Fran agreed on one thing. Marriage should be a gradual thing, not entered lightly. They would be sensitive to each other's scars. They would move cautiously. They could see living together as a way of avoiding mistakes and as a way to build up the trust and self-esteem they'd lost in their earlier experiences.

Interpreting the Three Relationships

These three marriages are only beginning, and it is impossible to predict how they will work out. But their beginnings are quite different. The "infancy" elements—dependency, basic trust, and views of world, self, and others—appear to blend in different ways.

Allen and Barbara are older and more educated when they marry. They have a better start on their chosen life goals. Their self-knowledge has had a chance to increase, and with it their capacity for intimacy. Neither time nor distance seems to weaken their relationship. Because Allen and Barbara can enter each other's individual worlds, marriage can be more continuous with their earlier lives. Their respective families can join the celebration without intruding on their new life together. Allen and Barbara are giving birth to a relationship under circumstances that are, statistically speaking, most favorable.

Charlie and Donna start out with convention and tradition on their side. Theirs is the kind of marriage that has been quite typical of the last several generations in America. Their backgrounds are similar, as are their schooling and work goals. Their lives are tied to family and community, but in ways that are within their control. Their sense of self and other is less individualistic and more conventional than that of Allen and Barbara. But their hopes are high, their potential good.

Eddie and Fran have had the rockiest start. They feel some lingering scars from what they perceive as earlier failures. Younger and less experienced in the world than the other couples, Eddie and Fran still struggle with self-identity and self-esteem. And they do so alone, without the benefit of networks from school, work, family or friends. Their need for intimacy is greater, while their confidence in their ability to offer intimacy is less.

They proceed with caution and tentativeness, bordering on fear of commitment. Their most important asset is the determination to make a relationship work this time.

In each later chapter, we will look in on our three couples to find out how they deal with the further stages of their relationships. But now is the time to look at the first stage of a marriage in its most positive and creative light: as the experience of *eros*.

Eros and the Importance of the Infancy Stage of Marriage

This chapter began with the suggestion that both stable and unstable marriages start out with the same structural similarities: attraction, sharing of selves and self-knowledge, desire for continued life together. Couples differ, of course, in the intensity of attraction. Their capacity to reveal themselves depends on the extent of their self-knowledge. And the depth of their desire for continuity has to do with their basic sense of trust in loving itself. In looking for possible explanations for these differences, we have turned to the developmental stages of infancy and early childhood to see if they suggest some helpful analogies. By thinking through the themes of dependency—basic trust, wonder, bonding, naive realism, and sacrifice—we can sharpen our sense that love is like a growth process, a series of changing patterns of reality, an unfolding of consciousness.

The concept of *eros* proves helpful in holding together in our minds the various aspects of the infancy stage of loving. *Eros* embraces thoughts about attraction, desire, longing, satisfaction, fulfillment—the experiences that are present from the very beginnings of a relationship right on through to the final stages. *Eros* reminds us of how closely the emotions of falling in love seem to parallel or recapitulate our earliest parent-child needs.

In the least stable relationships, *eros* is expressed as the search for a parent figure in order to complete the nurturing process. Often when young people grow up in destructive home conditions, their search for a mate takes on the aspects of the search for a better parent. When two such people find each other, the results can be tragically disappointing. A desperate search to be rescued reduces *eros* to a child-parent desire.

Even more tragically, a person may despair of finding another person to meet the deepest needs. Then the search trails off away from people altogether. Subhuman dependencies on alcohol, drugs, overeating, or overworking are the result. Here *eros* becomes a soul-destroying force. Only when the awareness of the destructiveness hits home hard enough is it possible to return to the pilgrimage of love.

An erotic-addictive relationship with a person or a substance is a tragic but all too familiar sight that tends to feed on itself. The partners cannot let go of each other. The psychological forces that hold them are coming from their earliest infancy experiences, with little help provided from their later life. It is very difficult to make any improvement by going back and getting in touch with early experiences, since the memory was not sufficiently developed to store any retrievable information. In spite of all the difficulties, thousands of people have freed themselves from dependencies and addictions through personal effort, group support, and effective counseling. These persons serve as reminders that even the worst retreats into infantile coping methods can be coaxed back onto the road to maturity.

For the average couple, in contrast, *eros* is a creative force that builds intimacy, pleasure, and trust. The couple's dependencies on each other are mutual, in balance, and strengthening. The main difficulty many couples face is that they are not as aware of the dynamics of dependency as they might be. Needless barriers to communication go up. Needless fears about losing control or being thought immature stifle the full range of erotic exploration.

In the healthiest relationships, *eros* embraces the sexual, emotional, intellectual, and spiritual yearnings of two people for each other. *Eros* offers a unifying force for intimacy of sight, sound, touch, word, thought, memory. The desires for sexual union fuse into a celebration of work and play. The longing for intercourse translates fantasies and dreams into values and goals. *Eros* cannot be understood as merely an ignition switch for love. The healthiest relationships maintain an erotic basis from the very beginning and experience it in an astonishing variety of permutations in later stages.

For this reason most relationships do not stabilize in Stage One. Other forces are calling the participants to advance into richer, more complex, more satisfying ways of experiencing love. But in making the transition to Stage Two, a couple must first undergo a period of disequilibrium. Stage One patterns begin to dissolve. Some couples in the throes of disorienting change mistake it for the death of the relationship itself. Divorce seems to be the only way out. Others experience the same degree of upheaval, but something tells them that this "divorce" is only a prelude to deeper loving. What this something is will be the theme of the next chapter.

Getting in Touch with Dependency

Here are some ways two people can become more aware of the important continuing influences of their early years together.

1. Recall to each other how you first met. Note the similarities and the differences in the details you remember.

2. What made this relationship different from others? Again note the similarities and differences in your memories.

3. Think back on the experiences that led you to want to marry this person. Does each of you recall the same kinds of experiences, or different ones?

4. Share with each other a memorable early time of lovemaking. (It doesn't matter whether you choose to recall two different occasions or the same one.) Be aware of the differences and similarities in what made the experience memorable.

5. As you've surfaced these early memories, see if you can find any patterns in the similarities and differences of your recollections. Do these patterns continue to influence the ways you view your experiences today?

The following explorations can help two people be more sensitive to the impact of their own earliest childhoods, and the ways their parents helped set up their ideas about loving.

1. Which parent does each of you feel you most resemble? In what ways, either positive or negative?

2. Which parent do you feel your spouse most resembles? In what ways, either positive or negative?

3. Which positive and negative elements in your parents' marriages do you see repeated in your own?

4. In what ways is your marriage quite different from those of each set of parents?

5. From what your parents have told you, what were the first two years of life like for each of you? (Were you healthy? Did you cry a lot? Was there outside pressure on the family?) If you can, refresh your memories by talking with a parent or someone else who remembers your early childhood.

41

6. What conclusions about the continuing influence in your marriage might you draw from your parents' marriages and from your earliest years of life?

Selected Reading for Background and Discussion

Stage One

Dependency, Infatuation and *Eros* in a Relationship

John Powell, *Why Am I Afraid to Tell You Who I Am?*
John Powell, *The Secret of Staying in Love*
Keith Miller, *Please Love Me*
Mircea Eliade, *Myths, Dreams and Mysteries*
Mircea Eliade, *Cosmos and History*
Emile Durkheim, *The Elementary Forms of Religious Life*
Burton White, *The First Three Years of Life*
Jean Piaget, *The Child and Reality*
D. Winton Thomas, ed., *Documents from Old Testament Times*
Kenneth Clark, *Civilization*

Storm

Stage Two: *Storge*, Love by the Rules
The Childhood Period of a Relationship

[*Storge*] lives with humble, undress, private things;
soft slippers, old clothes, old jokes,
the thump of a sleepy dog's tail on the kitchen floor. . . .
There is indeed a peculiar charm,
both in Friendship and in Eros,
about those moments when [Storge] love lies,
as it were, curled up asleep,
and the mere ease and ordinariness
of the relationship . . . wraps us round.
     No need to talk.
     No need to make love.
     No needs at all
     except perhaps to stir the fire.
     —C. S. Lewis, *The Four Loves*[3]

There are . . . men and women who experience
a strong sexual attraction for each other,
conclude they are "in love," and proceed to marry
on the basis of their sexual attraction,
ignoring the fact that they have
few values or interests in common,
have little or no genuine admiration for each other,
are bound to each other
predominantly by dependency needs,

have incompatible personalities and temperaments,
and, in fact, have little or no authentic interest
in each other as persons.
Of course such relationships
are doomed to failure.
> —Nathaniel Branden, *The Psychology of Romantic Love*[4]

The dependency stage of a marriage is only a temporary one for most couples. Only a few maintain a lifelong relationship in Stage One. Those who do most likely are trying to hold on to a security they never found in childhood. Happy to be safe from the early fears, they cling appreciatively to each other. Compared to the past, their present stability is such an improvement that the lure of an even better future is faint indeed.

The great majority of relationships grow beyond this earliest stage. Not that many of us would want to lose the gifts we received there—the electricity of attraction and infatuation, the rhythms of erotic and sensual desire, the heady ecstasy of falling in love. But the very power of these gifts creates a dilemma. A taste of intimacy creates a hunger for more. And for there to be more, with the same person, there must be continuity, stability, permanency.

For some couples, a contradiction appears between ecstasy and permanency. Much of the delight of attraction flows from its mystery and wonder and magic. So the period of settling in together extinguishes the flame.

Often this is the first severe test of a relationship: learning how to integrate the need for intimacy and the need for stability. A prolonged period of disequilibrium follows. Some marriages do not make it across this threshold. Divorce results. The search for ecstasy may continue, but with a variety of partners. Sometimes couples do not understand the natural and inevitable disequilibrium, and they mistake it for permanent failure. These couples, too, may decide to divorce, confusing mere growing pains with the death of the relationship.

Those who do make it across the threshold between infatuation and continuity often discover—to their surprise and joy—the arrival of a richer, deeper, more satisfying and more challenging stage of their marriage.

44

Establishing the roles and rules is a real challenge, no matter how mature the partners may be. The roles have to do with assignments: who will be breadwinner(s), who will pay the bills, clean the house, take care of the yard, fix things when they break. The rules have to do with acceptable performance: how much time is given to careers, how much money is earned, how often and how well the house is cleaned, the bills paid, repairs made.

Then there is the challenge of meshing two different temperaments:

—He is a morning person, wide awake at dawn. She is a late bloomer, hitting her stride about sundown.

—He's compulsively tidy, and she's, well, "very informal."

—When under pressure he tends to sulk, while she handles stress by letting it all out at the top of her lungs.

—He's sexually aggressive, while she's quietly manipulative.

Very quickly couples discover there are no easy sets of rules and roles to follow. In fact, the problem is too many sets to choose from. Their own parents and older siblings offer a variety of examples, even in the most traditional homes. In some families paying the bills is the breadwinner's prerogative, while in others it is the duty of the homemaker. And in two-career marriages, the roles are divided in a bewildering variety of ways. Today, there seem to be no rules for setting the rules.

When we stop and focus on the processes by which couples decide how to handle these essential yet mundane activities, it makes us wonder how anyone ever manages to work it out smoothly. The underlying question, from the standpoint of stage theory, is: Where do couples find the resources for negotiating a satisfactory settlement? What personality traits and values make for the establishment of roles and rules that are firm enough to depend on, yet flexible enough to meet changing needs?

There is a place to look, unlikely as it may seem at first glance, for the resources that are so essential in this second stage of marriage. And that place is the age of childhood.

Childhood: The Discovery of Roles and Rules

When we were infants, as we saw in our survey of Stage One, we perceived reality as a series of fluid, unpredictable situations. As time went on, however, we began to get our first sense that life runs in an orderly process. Our mental development made possible a new understanding of life as a series of events, predictable and dependable. Our earlier fears of being abandoned diminished, as did our need for the physical presence of a parent. Once we were able to feel secure even in the absence of our parents, we gained a sense of security through repeated experiences of calling out and getting a response.

If we could go back in time to our years from age four to eight, we would see that we were learning for the first time to make a distinction between the ordinary and the extraordinary, between the real and the unreal, between the private fantasy life that was going on inside the mind and the public reality that other people shared. We were beginning to observe behavior and to find patterns in it. Those were the years when we first made the attempt to describe how an event took place, to try to recall it, to hold it in the mind, and to retell it as a past experience. The earlier world of wonder and magic was beginning to change. Around it was growing a reality with which we could interact and partially control.

A person can be said to leave infancy when he or she learns to make sense of events. If one day simply blends into another, if the immediate moment is the only reality, if the memory cannot teach lessons from the past, then a person will remain infantile in some critically important ways. And relationships will remain dependent without adding the capacity to develop continuity through adopting roles and rules.

Learning to Develop Categories

At some point in early childhood, we became aware of our family's similarities and differences with the neighbors, the other kids at school, the people at church. Differences became visible between people who fit our family norm and those who did not. We were developing the capacity to use classifications and categories, and to apply these skills to the world around us.

In learning to make these distinctions, there may have been times when we could be pretty clumsy, even harsh. It's common for young children to discover differences in skin color, weight, handicaps, birth defects. Our parents will tell us about embarrassments we caused in pointing out these differences in public. Their embarrassments probably caused them to try to stifle these attempts on our part to distinguish between who we are and who others are.

On the other hand, most parents have done a lot of things right in helping us develop a sense of similarity and difference. They may have helped us find our place in our families by letting us spend time with relatives and showing us photos of distant kin and heirlooms from our ancestors. They may have shared their own childhoods with us by telling us stories and by showing us old toys, clothes, and pictures. And our parents may have spent time developing a close family identity, not only through the memorable experiences of family vacations and special ways of celebrating holidays, but also through their involvement in religious and community life. All these experiences were preparing us to become distinctive individuals who can function in a larger environment, crucial traits for handling the negotiations necessary for beginning our own families.

Games and Stories: Preparing for Empathy

In learning to understand and accept other points of view, some of our most valuable help came from the games we played and the stories we heard. Games and stories allowed us to put ourselves in other times and places, to try on other roles, to adopt different personas and test their effects. Our games and stories helped us prepare for empathy by letting us experience its precursor, imitative behavior.

Empathy develops out of physical imitation of an experience as a child perceives it. If a child sees his parents arguing, the child may start shouting. Even when the parents are simply calling loudly to each other from one room to another, the effect on the child may be the same. The child's shout reproduces that of the parents in volume but not in understanding.

An intermediate stage between imitation and empathy occurs when a child imitates the emotions as well as the actions of others. Suppose a child hears an adult say in a calm voice, "Your little friend Susie is crying because her doggie got hit by a car." If the child is not yet able to envision the event and its impact on Susie, there may not be a full comprehension of what happened. But if the child actually sees Susie crying, then the power of suggestion, or what is called the mimetic impulse, may lead the child to cry. But true mental empathy must come at a later stage,

47

when the child can respond just as fully to a mental image of an event as to the event itself.

Sometimes adults who are trapped in dependent relationships remain incapable of true empathy. Their love is on an "out of sight, out of mind" level. A popular song a few years ago poked fun at this lack of love for the absent lover with the words, "If you can't be with the one you love, love the one you're with."

Our games and stories help us develop from imitation to empathy. By playing house, or cops and robbers, we were performing roles in a drama, complete with stage, costumes, and lines. We started by imitating behavior we had witnessed in others. But the games got more creative as we invented dialogue and developed new plots, episodes, and endings.

Fairy tales and stories also helped us move back and forth between fact and fantasy. The stories we liked best were the ones in which we could identify with characters who were struggling with our struggles, finding solutions we could live with. It's no accident that our most beloved fairy tales were about children left alone to cope with big scary forces. We identified with Hansel and Gretel, Goldilocks, or Little Red Riding Hood. The fear of abandonment and rejection by all-powerful parents or stepparents who don't really have our interests at heart reaches deeply into the heart of a child.

As we learn to tell stories about our own lives, the sense of control over mysterious forces grows even more. As small children, we might have heard a parent telling about something interesting at work. As far as we were concerned, that parent was telling a story. The distinction between fiction and nonfiction would be lost on us. We might come in and tell our parents about a fight the dolls just had, and it would be just as real and true as the one our parents told about the office.

The effect of games and stories on our later potential for intimate relationships is rich and profound. By involving ourselves in a variety of fantasies, we learned to make sense of the world and of our place in it. By becoming involved with others in shared play activities and by hearing stories known to millions, we knew we were not alone in our feelings. We found that when other people shared their feelings with us, their anxieties and our own were not quite so threatening. When our parents read to us and talked to us, they were preparing us to trust the communica-

48

tion process as a way of solving problems and removing barriers to understanding and intimacy. To the extent that we were deprived of a childhood full of games and stories, we may still be struggling with distinctions between the real world and our fantasies. It may seem paradoxical, but the more we explored imaginary worlds, the better prepared we became to face the real world. And the more we were deprived of a rich imagination, the less we can trust our ideas, our goals, our words.

Learning to Express Feelings

Another important transition, which took years in developing, was the blending of words as well as cries to communicate our needs. As infants, our cries were the main vehicles of communication. Even then, we developed a whole range of cries that varied with our needs. Later we prided ourselves on being able to use words as well as vocal sounds, and gave ourselves a new, highly versatile, and powerful way of getting on in the world. Sometimes we blended both words and cries to say, "Daddy! Come here! I fell down and hurt myself!"

The ability to express feelings has its origins in this childhood stage. If this capacity has been blocked or delayed, we may find difficulty later in blending our feelings and our words. Some of us may struggle to articulate our feelings in words, while others of us find our emotions themselves to be the problem, either underreacting (being unable to weep or laugh appropriately) or overreacting (uncontrollable anger or physical violence). It may require a great deal of practice before feelings can be blended with words. One way to speed up the process is to become more involved in stories and games on an adult level—to take up a sport, see more plays, good movies, and TV drama—to go back and recapture those less threatening, more innocent childhood times when the resources for expressing feelings first became available. These seemingly unconnected activities can often enhance the expression of feelings in a relationship and facilitate growth well beyond what would be possible when working only directly with the problem itself.

Learning to Develop Preferences

Our powers of discrimination are also given to us for the first time in our childhood experiences. The development of individual taste is a sign of our individuality. Children quickly gain a preference for certain kinds of foods, items of clothing, games, and even TV shows, which, if not ridiculed or stifled by parents or other family members, can lead to growth in decision-making ability. Sometimes the food choices may not be nutritious ones. Clothing choices may not always conform to adult ideas or even seasonal appropriateness. It takes patience and wisdom on the part of a parent to guide a child through the process, especially when the child invariably chooses cake over vegetables. Parents have to produce commercials in favor of nutritional food that are as interesting and persuasive as the ones the child sees on TV to sell snacks.

Eventually a child must become a sophisticated member of the consumer society, knowing how to make choices and develop preferences that are in the individual's best interest, not necessarily in the interest of the seller of a product. Sadly, some adults were stifled by their parents in their childhood years, protected from the consequences of their own decisions. However well-meaning, such overprotectiveness may simply delay a person's capacity to make decisions in his or her own best interests. The impact on a person's ability to choose those with whom to build a relationship can be devastating. Too often, delayed capacity for developing personal preferences results in years of pitched battles, willfulness, even rebelliousness as the person tries to make up for lost time and overcompensates. It's safe to say that the better the early environment was for decision making and the more affirmation that was given for the right to hold an opinion, the better prepared a person will be for trusting one's judgment in the all-important area of relationships.

Looks Are All-Important to the Child-Mind

As children we responded to other people first on the basis of physical appearance and only much later for their personal qualities. We looked up to policemen, nurses, doctors, football players, cowboys, soldiers. Their uniforms made them stand out, as did their props—the motorcycle, the hospital, the stadium, the corral, the battlefield. It was the powerful physical impression that created a sense of awe in us. And that was the beginning of our development of a set of values. Size and power were at the top of the list for us.

50

One four-year-old was asked how his daddy learned the difference between right and wrong. The little boy answered, "Well, some lady that's bigger than him probably told him." (Which was probably true; the father's own mother was that lady.) The child, however, did not envision a time when his father was a boy.

To some extent, we never outgrow this tendency to tie our values to size, power, and physical appearance. But relationships that are based on looks above all else indicate an arrested sense of values. The capacity to admire less tangible and more personal qualities appears only in later childhood.

Appearances and Motives

One important threshold to cross in childhood is that of judging behavior on the basis of motive rather than mere appearance.

Researchers have documented how the shift takes place. First they show children a film that features two children attempting to wash dishes. In one scene, a child is at the sink, standing precariously on a stool. The soapy dishes are slippery, and she accidentally drops one. Later she drops another, and still another, until four or five dishes are accidentally broken. In the second scene, another child comes into the kitchen and she's mad about something. She reaches into the sink, picks up a beautiful pitcher, and hurls it to the ground.

The researcher then asks the children who have viewed the film which of the two girls will get into the most trouble. Most children say that the one who broke the most dishes will be punished the most. For them, size and number are the standards for right and wrong behavior. Some young viewers, however, note that one child consciously and intentionally broke the pitcher, and that accidents are not as bad as purposeful misbehaving.

This discovery of the idea of motive is a major advance of childhood, and is taken for granted by most adults as they evaluate behavior in relationships. Some adults, however, never make the complete passage. They often make judgments based on superficial observations:

"I saw the way you were looking at him."

"It was nine o'clock when you came home from work last night."

"Of course, she's been married twice before, you know."

"You never cook my favorite foods anymore."

If the person making these statements were challenged about the judgments inherent in them, we might hear a protest: "All I said was. . . . " Many times persons given to such statements are unaware that they have rolled up facts, accusations, verdicts, and assessments of punishment into their "harmless" comments. But these comments reflect an inability to separate fact from motive, and they can be deadly to a relationship.

To summarize: One of the most liberating things we discovered as children was that the world runs by predictable rules we can count on. The sun will always come up tomorrow. Learning to talk gives us power over our environment and a closer relationship with our parents and friends. Playing games and listening to stories enrich our understanding of the real world and help us practice preparing to take our place in it. Having our favorite foods and our favorite heroes prepared us to believe in the rights of others to their own opinions. We were learning to interact with our environment, being neither passive and helpless nor omnipotent and tyrannical. We were learning the proper place for roles and rules in developing healthy relationships.

Our Roots in the Childhood Period of Culture

It seems clear that when two people enter into a relationship, they are influenced by the resources they bring from their own childhoods. What may be equally as important is the influence of the culture around us in determining which of our early values are emphasized and which are relegated to the background. The fact is that our cultural values can be judged in terms of their maturity or immaturity just as significantly as can the development of our personalities.

It may be helpful if we try to imagine that our culture has gone through stages of growth and that there is evidence of a childhood stage of culture. From it the values of Stage Two marriage may have first developed.

This childhood stage of culture emerged perhaps two thousand years before Christ, when the most advanced civilizations were breaking away from more primitive practices of living. All over the ancient world, different groups were emerging from a fearful, superstitious sense of being at the mercy of nature. They

52

were moving away from the view of life that saw all the power being held by mysterious, unpredictable gods, who demand sacrifice without giving anything in return.

In this emerging stage of culture, a different view of the world was being adopted. People were learning how to control nature and to cooperate with it, to plant seeds and harvest crops, to domesticate animals and use them for work, to settle in fertile areas and develop village life, to bring stability to family, tribe, and community life through laws and customs regarding marriage, property inheritance, and protection from outside attacks.

These discoveries and inventions can be seen as byproducts of a new awareness that the world runs by predictable rules which can be determined and then used to our benefit. About the same time that early civilization was developing an appreciation for the laws of nature, the first and most powerful religions based on law appeared. These were the faiths that promised rewards for good behavior and penalties for wrongdoing. During this time, life came to be seen as the gift of the one Creator God. Unlike the unpredictable, capricious, and even dangerously immoral gods of primitive belief, this God revealed himself as trustworthy and dependable. The God who assures that the sun rises and sets, that the seasons follow in their courses, that seedtime and harvest will continue, is also a God who makes promises in his relationship to human beings. And quite apart from the cruel nature of the primitive gods, this God has our best interests at heart and has revealed the secrets of our well-being, the laws that will provide our greatest happiness.

As people learned the laws of cultivation, pruning, and harvest, they applied these same rules to human behavior: cultivating the good, pruning the bad, in anticipation of the ultimate harvest.

These times also saw the rise of the earliest forms of lifelong marriage and the system of laws that would protect and enhance continuity in life. The laws of primogeniture (inheritance by the eldest son) and of matriarchy or patriarchy (the carrying on of the mother's or father's name and lineage) date from this period of history. Looking back from this distance, it is easy to take for granted our inheritance and to criticize it for its treatment of women and of younger sons, and for its stark and severe limitations on domestic love. At the same time, we owe this period a great debt for giving us the concept of legal protections for love;

the first guarantees for generational families, property, and homes; the first divisions of labor; the first written communications; and the first religious values that placed the love between God and God's people as the highest good.

The Three Couples

It's tempting to suppose that all this emphasis on social and personal background gives us too much of a backward look. The real focus, of course, is growth in our relationships *today*. It's not enough to be aware of our *sources*; the point is that our sources are our greatest *resources.* To see the way it works, let's look in again on our three couples, Allen and Barbara, Charlie and Donna, Eddie and Fran.

For *Allen and Barbara*, their basic trust in themselves and in each other remains very high. Even though their courtship and early days of marriage were very intense, they still sense there is much more to know about each other. They look forward to building their careers and sharing their interests. Both of them love children and are looking forward to being parents. They don't intend to simply "work it into their schedules," nor do they see children as necessary interruptions to satisfying careers. So they are at work on a solution that would involve considerable fathering from Allen—he works at home—and a more flexible schedule for Barbara in her activities on behalf of political candidates.

One serious problem has arisen between them. Sexually, Allen has begun to feel that he has to take the initiative far more often than he'd like. And Barbara, perhaps in self-defense, finds it increasingly harder to be open, spontaneous, and comfortable around Allen, particularly as it gets closer to bedtime. She'd like to feel she could have a little of his time and attention without setting in motion an inevitable, predictable series of events that end in a routine of sex with the lights out.

Eventually they started talking it over with a counselor—after Barbara took the scary first step of asking a friend to recommend someone. The counselor's opinion was that both Allen and Barbara were trying to cope with a mutual fear of losing control. Allen's technique, unconscious to be sure, was to beat Barbara to the draw. His fear of losing control was getting in the way of his need for intimacy and affection. Barbara, in contrast, resolved her anxieties by withdrawing from the field: You can't lose if you don't play.

Once they realized they both were struggling with the same problem, Allen and Barbara felt closer to each other than they had for a long time. It was a relief to find out that their differences in temperament were not going to throw up a barrier. They have begun talking to each other about their fears of being controlled, what they do to arouse each other's fears, and what they can do to still them. Sometimes the conversation opens a space where they can make love to each other; sometimes their talks feel good just by themselves.

If *Charlie and Donna* knew Allen and Barbara, they'd think such talk about "control" and "anxiety" was a lot of wasted energy. Charlie and Donna love each other a lot. They look forward to the end of the day when they can be together. Each of them works hard all day. Donna is now assistant manager of a nearby Dairy Queen. Charlie is developing some group insurance policies among small companies in the area, which will mean more travel in the short run, a more lucrative agency in the long run. It's going to be tough for awhile. Some of their friends are already beginning to file for divorce. But not Charlie and Donna. They've worked too hard for what they've got. They believe they can gut it up and tough it out.

Yet Charlie and Donna keep running into a brick wall whenever an argument threatens to break out. That's the problem: They don't argue. Oh, Donna's more than willing to get things out in the open. Charlie's the one who refuses to get involved. Whenever he's upset about something, Charlie turns on the TV, dumps himself into the recliner, picks up the paper, and escapes into a world created by filmmakers and sportswriters. That doesn't quiet Donna, though. Just the opposite. Nothing angers her more quickly than watching Charlie's mind disappear over the horizon. And so goes the evening. An hour of "static electricity buildup," followed by an instant violent charge that stuns them both. It's getting so that some pretty serious problems are in need of heavy-duty negotiation. But it's not happening.

If Charlie and Donna knew *Eddie and Fran*, they'd be upset to find out that this couple has been living together for over a year, and still aren't married. Eddie and Fran call it "this thing we've got going." Even so, they're both very proud of their relationship. It's the most important part of their life, the most satisfying time either of them has ever known. Eddie keeps food on the table with a variety of odd jobs. Fran takes care of children in the neighborhood kids for "working mothers." The two have few really close friends, but frequently someone they know will call and ask to come spend a couple of days. Often it's somebody who's had an argument at home. Eddie and Fran are becoming known for always having a place where one can stay (their living room couch). They can offer a little breakfast and a lot of understanding. They sympathize with anybody who's trying to keep a relationship going against difficult odds. Sometimes Eddie and Fran resent the interference with their time together, but they're pleased that others look to them as a force to lean on.

There is one problem lurking in the shadows. It hasn't been discussed much because it seems unimportant. The trouble is, Fran's child care activities occupy all the open areas of their small house—living room, eating area, kitchen, hallways, and the bathroom. At the end of the day the house looks like—well, like half a dozen preschoolers were let loose in it for nine hours. Eddie tries to be understanding, and he's not terribly neat himself, but he's beginning to dread coming home after work. He's started stopping off for a "Happy Hour" drink "to give Fran a little more time to straighten up." He hasn't said much about it because he knows Fran is trying.

Making Adjustments

Each of these three couples is coming to terms with a problem common to Stage Two of a relationship. In this stage two people find that their daily routines need to mesh. Much of their energy goes into making little compromises and adjustments in their habits—and in their expectations of what it is like to share the same space.

Most of the adjustments work out without a lot of strain, but a few problems usually arise that demand more attention. Problems of temperament, for example, take more work than problems of habits.

Allen and Barbara ran up against a sexual problem. Such problems can be severely troubling in early marriage, especially when the reality falls far short of expectations. Even worse, sexual conflict usually conceals problems somewhere else in the relationship, problems that are harder to surface and treat. Thus, the decision to seek counseling at this early stage in the marriage demonstrates exceptional and rare maturity. Most couples wait until their problems get much worse before seeking outside help, for most of us have been trained to work things out for ourselves. We view counseling as a last resort, and we view people who seek early counseling with suspicion if not alarm. In truth, the counseling that is sought early in the marriage quite often decreases the problem areas later in the relationship.

In seeking counseling, Allen and Barbara were fortunate enough to discover something important. Allen's sexual aggressiveness and Barbara's passivity were not signs of incompatibility, but of differing reactions to the same problem. Instead of letting the problem drive them farther apart, they found a way to let the problem bring them closer together.

Charlie and Donna, on the other hand, have a head start over the other two couples in many areas belonging to Stage Two. They mesh well in their work goals, scheduling of their day, and activities together after work. They are even compatible on the issue of how to settle conflicts. They agree not to press each other. Neither of them seems to realize, however, that conflicts delayed cause more trouble than conflicts confronted. They are buying their current compatibility on the installment plan, and someday the bill will come due. When it does, they may lack the experience to deal with the big crises because they failed to get enough practice with the smaller ones.

As for Eddie and Fran, some serious incompatibilities already are burrowing into their relationship, serious enough to be life-threatening, though they see none of it yet. Not even the basic strengths of a Stage Two marriage are protecting Eddie and Fran at this point. They are still caught in the dilemma of what to call their relationship, how far to trust each other, how far to accept personal responsibility. It's a conditional relationship—for better but not for worse. There will be little room for any serious setbacks or even any lengthy holding patterns, although all healthy growth requires periods of both equilibrium and disequilibrium that might easily be mistaken for signs that the relationship is sick or even dying.

Another dilemma is that they seem to be unwilling to have children at this point, yet their house is full of them day and night—the children of other parents during the day and children masquerading as adults at night.

Finally, and most serious, is the indication that Eddie has already found a way to deal with his problem in a way that doesn't include Fran. If he continues using the "Happy Hour" as his way of coping, it will begin demanding more and more from him while delivering less and less, until his solution becomes the problem.

Storge: The Place of Affection

The combined personal and cultural emphasis on a world of law bequeaths to every one of us a wide range of resources for maintaining our personal relationships. When we understand the importance of the orderly processes in life, we can better appreciate the importance of ordinary, everyday experiences for the growth of a relationship. The ancient Greeks, as we've seen, had a word for it: *storge, domestic love, affection, the love of the familiar. Storge* is the love that emerges in the stage of domesticity in a relationship. It is expressed in the simple joys of being together.

In the second stage of your love relationship, you develop an appreciation of the ordinary moments you spend together as well as the extraordinary moments. You can *like* being together without *needing* to. The earlier insecurities and dependencies have receded. The fear of being abandoned no longer arises, and the time you spend apart no longer breeds fear or suspicion. When you are together you are comfortable carrying out routine tasks; when you are apart, you are free to assume your daily responsibilities.

Stage Two is a settling-in process. You're engaged in the work of meshing the routines and habits of daily living that each of you has brought to the marriage. Your early experiences as children learning the rules of human relations come into play, as do the values you bring from your religious and cultural environment, particularly those that offer resources for playing (and living) by the rules of orderly and fair behavior. If your early experiences and your social background have prepared you adequately, the two of you can start setting goals together and settling on the roles each of you needs to pay to achieve them.

The Stage Two influences from childhood and culture in large measure determine which roles each of you will play. Roles, at this point in your relationship, offer you positive elements. Like the imagery of dramatics from which the idea of role-playing originates, roles in a marriage help separate who I am from what I do. The distinction is an advance over Stage One where, as in the dependency and helplessness of infancy, one *is* before one *does* anything. To play a role is to assume a temporary identity in terms of what one does, without destroying the actual identity of who one is. That's why lovers can *play* roles such as breadwinner, housekeeper, mechanic, grocery shopper, bill payer, lawnkeeper, gardener, and so on.

The "First Divorce": Becoming Type-cast in Your Roles

If your roles become identities, and if you start feeling trapped by roles instead of feeling free to define yourself outside of them, then it's time for some serious renegotiation of who's supposed to do what in your marriage. If the two of you were able to navigate your early childhood periods without undue delays or pressure to move out too quickly, you will be able to communicate ideas for changes in your roles. You will be able to express both positive and negative feelings.

If either or both of you spent too little time or too much in your childhood emotional stage, you may find it hard even now to express negative feelings. One of the first "rules" you learned as a child was "Stop crying!" Learning some control of your emotions is a necessary part of Stage Two consciousness, but it can be overdone. If you are blocked off from your deepest feelings, your "control" is out of control. Sometimes you have to decide to remove the controls and let the feelings flow. That takes even more maturity.

How You Got Your House Rules

In Stage Two of a marriage, each of you looks to the other for authentication of your feelings. No longer is this done out of insecurity or dependency, but as a means of gaining information for making comparisons. As you mutually develop your personal preferences, and as you make your decisions, the patterns begin to emerge for your house rules and regulations. (Every couple has them. Some are aware of what they are, and some are not.)

The rules and roles established by most couples will reflect one degree or another of moral and rational content. If your childhood experience was of rules enforced by power ("Because I said so") you will tend to try to enforce your wills upon each other. But if your parents' rules were blended with moral reasoning, you will experience the settling-in stage as an opportunity for calm discourse and sensitivity for each other's needs.

What role does a person's childhood religious training play in later relationships? The crucial factor probably is not whether your upbringing was "strict" or "tolerant." What is decisive is whether your parents were deeply caring or apathetic about spiritual realities. A caring environment, whether strict or tolerant, closed or open, plants the seeds of a later capacity for setting high goals, for trusting people deeply, for daring to dream. An early uncaring environment later reinforces unpredictable, arbitrary, suspicious behavior. Insecure couples often are afraid to make promises and don't trust their ability (or that of others) to keep them. Keeping promises and making commitments stem from the basic trust in the dependability of life's processes learned from Stage Two experiences.

If as a child you developed a healthy attitude toward a fair system of rewards and penalties used by your parents, your abilities as an adult to set your priorities and follow them will be affected. Positive early experiences, with rewards and penalties, enable you as an adult to devise your own internal carrot-and-stick systems. You can become your own behavior modifiers. You can accept delayed gratification in your relationships, passing up short-term pleasures in favor of long-term benefits. You no longer confuse love and loss. You can accept sacrifice as a necessary and positive dynamic and can try to be sure you always sacrifice the lesser good for the greater. You can also build positive reinforcement into your scheduling of work, holding back your most pleasant activities as rewards for those unpleasant but necessary routines.

The way the two of you approach male and female roles is affected by your early training about the nature of God. If as a child you received no formal training about God, it is possible that you still view sex roles as ultimate categories, just as people did in prehistoric times. You may find that you tend to accept hard-and-fast masculine and feminine images (macho man, seductive woman) as normative. But the view of God as One who transcends male and female offers you a view of masculine and feminine roles as distinct from identities. Roles, after all, are for playing, not for defining your place in life. Couples who share this view may find that they can play roles without becoming identified with them.

Playing roles makes possible the division of labor, and a resulting efficiency of effort. Instead of viewing their biological roles as normative, Stage Two couples can subject their biological drives to service in behalf of personal, relational, and family values. The kinds of services a couple performs for each other can become specialized. The various roles each partner plays provide each with experience and expertise. The result of such specialization is more achievements for the amount of work expended. Roles thus allow couples to get more of their duties finished in less time and to have more time left to spend with each other.

Stage Two marriage, as you can see, is a very practical stage. Most of what it offers a couple has to do with working smoothly together, both in and outside the home. Stage Two has given us the so-called "work ethic." The goal, however, is not to see how hard the two of you can work but to see how efficiently, quickly, and easily you can get it all done. The new leisure time provided by the efficiency of role relationships has left many Stage Two couples looking for new meaning in life. If you have viewed your roles as ends in themselves, you may have trouble envisioning how to proceed in the free time you have given yourselves. All too often, a Stage Two couple simply take on extra work or new careers to fill up the time. They may eventually turn the work ethic into a stage of dependency, and become workaholics. Others, however, develop the awareness that leads them into a new, third stage of relating to each other.

In Stage Two, each day spent in working at the assigned duties is like one brick added in the construction of a wall. Each routine act is a symbol, a ritual, with meaning beyond itself. Each day's work is part of a larger goal. Because of the presence of an overarching purpose, the daily grind may strengthen your relationship and reaffirm the validity of your goals. For Stage Two couples, love is the sum of what you've been through together. Love is the experience of one thing after another. Because of this gradual adding of experience to experience, of adding one day to

61

another, you can build a strong wall against the pressures continually brought against you by the forces pulling you back toward Stage One.

Role marriage provides a place for the two of you in the order of things. Together you help each other withstand the forces of chaos. Role marriage provides a place where two people can come in from the cold. It offers a new appreciation for the glory of the ordinary. The thrills and suspense provided by the uncertainties of Stage One are seen for what they are: an immature response to the opportunities and potentials of a loving relationship. In the words of Antoine St. Exupery, the two lovers "stand side by side, looking out at the world together."

Talking Together About Roles and Rules

Every marriage passes through a stage where settling in together occupies the couple's energies. The rules and roles that characterize a relationship should not be ignored or despised. It's not possible to build a relationship without them. The first step toward getting the most out of a role marriage is to know its dynamics as thoroughly as possible. Communication often begins too late, after the rules and roles have become negative influences. But the two of you can examine and assess the dynamics of your own rules and roles by discussing frequently and openly the various ways your relationship is affected. To encourage each other to share vital information, and to form crucial insights about each other, you can start by comparing notes on your answers to questions such as the following:

1. How did each of your parents deal with the roles of breadwinner and housekeeper?

2. Which parent's role do you most admire? Least admire?

3. How many of the following roles do you play in your relationship: breadwinner, housekeeper, parent, church worker, friend, adviser, party giver, meal preparer, grocery shopper, repairer, lawn keeper, bill payer? Which of you is the primary actor in each of these roles? What other major roles would you add?

4. Which roles have you discussed and negotiated together? Which have you more or less assumed for yourself without considering alternatives?

5. Which of your roles are most satisfying to you? Which are least satisfying? Does your spouse know which are your most and least enjoyable roles? Do you know your spouse's most and least enjoyable roles?

6. How do you decide the way you will spend the evening? Spend your vacation? Spend your money?

7. What sounds like a pleasant evening at home to you? How does this compare with your partner's view?

8. Among your friends and people you admire, which couple divides its roles most like the way you do? Which couple's roles are most different from yours?

As the two of you discuss and analyze your roles, you can come to a clearer understanding of the processes, conscious or unconscious, that have led to the various divisions of labor in your marriage. You don't necessarily make big changes that would lead to role reversals or to the abolition of your roles. As long as you live together, you will follow certain rules and play certain roles. To make any significant impact on the nature of the roles in your marriage, you will need from time to time to look at yourselves from a fresh perspective. That new perspective is available in the two places we have learned to look: the early personal growth that each of you experienced, and the cultural values that have influenced each of you. Together these resources will prepare your way to a new level of love relationships.

This new level will unfold for you as you come to understand the Stage Three marriage in the next chapter.

Selected Reading for Background and Discussion

Stage Two

The Rise of Roles and Rules in History and Personality

Eric Berne, *Games People Play*
Thomas Harris, *I'm O.K., You're O.K.*
Paul Tournier, *Guilt and Grace*
Karl Menninger, *Whatever Became of Sin?*
G. E. Wright and Reginald Fuller, *The Book of the Acts of God*
William F. Albright, *From the Stone Age to Christianity*
John Bright, *A History of Israel (Third Edition)*
Virginia Satir, *Peoplemaking*

Stage Three:
Philia, Love as Friendship
The Pre-Adolescent Period of a Relationship

He is altogether desirable.
This is my beloved,
and this is my friend,
O daughters of Jerusalem.
—*Song of Solomon 5:16*

In Iran women are expected to be practical and cool
while men are emotional, sensitive, intuitive.
The Tutsi of Africa consider women "naturally" stronger.
Among the Navajo and Hopi tribes, one considers weaving men's work
and pottery making only for women, while the other tribe
declares the reverse to be "natural."
—Letha Scanzoni and Nancy Hardesty, *All We're Meant to Be*[5]

In every marriage there comes a time when the difficult work
of settling on the roles and rules of survival has been completed as
well as the couple can do it. The partners have kept their roles
separate from their identities. They have negotiated their rules
rather than assuming them, and have kept the rules flexible and
simple.

Once they've done their work as well as they can, couples begin to sense the call to a different, better level of relating. The more successful their work in Stage Two, the more insistent the call. As the call grows louder, couples begin to see more clearly the limitations to the life offered by Stage Two. At some point a marriage defined by roles and rules threatens to bog people down into legalism.

The "Second Divorce": Becoming Trapped by Roles and Rules

Inevitably, a life controlled and dominated by roles and rules turns into something very different from the earlier experience of affection, settling in together, enjoying doing the simple things together. "Legalism" is a good term to describe the tendency to give higher value to roles and rules than to other aspects of the good life. Legalism almost always puts distance between people. There are several reasons for this:

1. *Legalism obscures the reality of growth stages.*

Because roles and rules are only the second stage of personality growth, it is hard for a person in Stage Two to see all the challenges that lie ahead. A person who has moved from Stage One to Stage Two has experienced only two growth stages that reinforce the tendency to view life as dualistic, as either/or.

2. *Legalism forces dependency on authority figures.*

In the childhood stage, we depend on authority figures to tell us right from wrong. If we retain this dependency on into adulthood, we will tend to rely on the presence of an authority figure to keep us on the right path. When this authority is out of sight, and we are on our own, we find that we have no well-developed inner moral code, except perhaps a memory of the voice of the authority. Legalism thus works against the internalization of moral values.

3. *Legalism confuses roles with identities.*

The term *identity* refers to the definition of Who I Am, while the term *role* refers to the description of What I Do. Even though many times we tend to confuse the two and to define our identities in terms of our careers or our relationships, we can never fully succeed. As our personalities develop, we become conscious of needs that cannot be met either by doing anything or by changing any of our roles. We cannot forget that roles are to be played, as in a drama, not absorbed into our identities like food into our bloodstream. Even our successful roles of breadwinner, parent, lover, are more like long-running Broadway hits; at some point our roles will end, and our identities remain.

4. *Legalism ignores shades of gray.*

In order to develop a sense of priorities, a person has to hold certain core values along with other important, yet not central, values. There are still other values of lesser importance that are nevertheless significant. In the world of legalism, values tend to become polarized as being either absolutely central or totally unimportant. A person is robbed of the sense of facing a range of choices. Actions are viewed as either essential or unimportant, whereas in reality most people can, for example, make a list of several things to do today and rank them in order of importance. Legalism often drives a person through guilt to feel like a failure unless every single item is completed, rather than to take satisfaction from each major accomplishment.

5. *Legalism encourages the loophole-seeking mentality.*

Many people whose personalities never transcend the stage of rules and roles find themselves trapped into looking for loopholes as their primary means of adapting to life's complexities. They still accept the right of rules and rulers to coerce them. But they look for technicalities they can use to get the authority figures to grant them exceptions. It is a way of refusing to take responsibility for the full range of personal choice. Under legalism a person can pick and choose the situations when he or she wants freedom. The securities of childhood can thus be prolonged throughout life, but at great cost.

6. *Legalism turns love into a tactic.*

The system of rewards and penalties often produces relationships that use the giving and withholding of love as a tactic rather than as an expression of personality. When love becomes a tool for manipulation, or a prop for a role, it loses its authentic intention. Using love as a tactic is like using a surgical knife to cut cardboard: once you misuse it, you can never again put it to its intended purpose.

7. *Legalism raises barriers to intimacy.*

If I offer my love as a reward, I can never be sure whether another person is responding to me or to the reward I'm offering. And if I withhold love as a penalty, I can never be sure the person I punish cares about me or is simply acting to avoid unpleasant consequences. The effect is to produce the opposite of what I intend: a relationship in which I am a traffic cop instead of a driver, a lifeguard instead of a swimmer, a referee instead of a player.

The negative effects of legalism over the years can numb us to the possibilities of change. At the same time, we may want desperately to find a way out of the traps of a Stage Two relationship. It is heartening to remind ourselves that the dynamics of change are always near at hand. Powerful resources are hidden within each one of us. All around us in our cultural environment are the influences from people through the centuries who have overcome the very problems we are facing. Once we become aware of these personality resources, and the environmental influences, we can then move into a welcome new stage of consciousness.

The Radical Idea of Marrying Your Best Friend

The fact is, happily, that nearly all of us have moved ahead, have outgrown the childhood period, and now face other needs in our love relationships. Simply calling for more rules or stricter observance of our roles will only make matters worse. As soon as these needs for roles and rules begin to be met, however, most of us find that a strange combination of boredom and anxiety begins to set in. Is this all there is? we wonder. Is this all I have to look forward to? It's kind of nice, and it's better than the old days with their unpredictability and constant struggle for security. But am I supposed to do it this way the rest of my life?

A lot of couples assume that Stage Two is all there is. You come home from work. You eat supper, watch TV, have sex in the dark, and go to sleep. More of the same tomorrow. And tomorrow. If people are happy doing this, I suppose we should let these sleeping relationships lie. But for most of us, the good news is that many complex forces are at work in our lives every day to draw us into a higher stage of consciousness. New challenges awaken hidden resources within us. It seems that as soon as we feel at home in Stage Two, our love begins to draw us into a new relationship, Stage Three, where life becomes more complex and demanding, but also more deeply satisfying.

The Three Couples

We can see our own situations more clearly as we see other couples dealing with the new forces in different ways.

Allen and Barbara found their relationship moving into Stage Three earlier than most of us. One of their first breakthroughs was the discovery of what to do about incompatible temperaments. When a counselor helped them see that Allen's sexual aggressiveness and Barbara's sexual passivity were differing ways of coping with the same fear of losing control, they were brought closer together on a deeper level. Since that first experience, Allen and Barbara have run into a number of other differences in temperament. They have resolved them with relaxed equanimity by looking for the common basis on which their differences rest. They in effect have come to realize that differing temperaments do not reflect differing stages of growth.

Since we last saw them, Allen and Barbara have become parents of a daughter, who is now six months old.

Before they made their decision to start a family, Allen and Barbara talked out a lot of feelings about the changes children might bring. Barbara talked about her fear of being stranded at home. She also knew she would love being at home with her child, and felt torn between her deeply rooted instincts for nurturing and for independence. Allen expressed his fear of getting stuck in a more traditional role, playing breadwinner to her housekeeper. He'd enjoyed a lot of freedom and flexibility up to now, doing his art work at home, and depending on Barbara's income to carry them through the times when his paintings weren't selling. For both of them, few walls had separated marriage and job, roles and identities, and now they were about to take on a new role that could upset the balance.

Now that their baby has arrived, Allen and Barbara are finding that parenting has deeply affected their lives in ways they never anticipated. Their outside activities have receded, and their child has created a momentum to life all her own.

Allen has begun turning out more commercially-appealing paintings, which give him more money and less creative satisfaction. This also gives him more time to help Barbara take care of the baby.

Barbara's time working on political activities has been curtailed, particularly her travel. She still works several hours a week in behalf of some issues she favors. She's become increasingly aware of how infant care has a special political dimension. Shopping for infant goods has opened her eyes to the commercial pressures facing young mothers to buy things that may not be in the best interest of babies but are profitable to corporations. Barbara has also started reading with more interest about the controversial sales of infant formula to Third World mothers who can neither read the directions nor use clean water.

Parenting, careers, and marriage seem to be relating well for Allen and Barbara. So far, they've made adjustments creatively, accepted tradeoffs realistically, and kept their eyes open for ways to overcome the pressures that remain.

Charlie and Donna. Charlie has started his own insurance agency and Donna has become store manager of the Dairy Queen. Their job-life keeps them busy and satisfied. They don't feel they have time yet for children, but they both want a family—especially Donna. She's always looked forward to being a mother. Charlie agrees and says he likes the idea of Donna's staying home and having a baby. He doesn't mind her working, even though it's not necessary now that his business is beginning to bring in big returns. He takes pride in the fact that he's providing so well.

Their main problem, though, is not about children, but parents. Hers. Donna's mother has started putting pressure on them to start coming to church again. Charlie and Donna haven't been to church much since they got married. They enjoy the rest on Sunday. Charlie, especially, doesn't know the people at the church where Donna grew up. And his parents were not regular churchgoers anyway.

They've talked about going to church, even to the point of noticing which churches in town their friends and associates attend. Donna's mother would expect them to go to the old family church, and she would probably be as disappointed for them to attend some other church as she would if they didn't go at all.

One night Donna and her mom had a big argument about church. Donna told her mother what she thought of the attitudes of the people at the church—they're too old, too set in their ways, too critical and too boring. Besides, Donna said with an air of finality, she didn't believe most of the things she was taught when she was growing up.

The rift still hasn't healed. And it certainly hasn't given parent-child relationships much of a boost.

Eddie and Fran. While Charlie and Donna are putting their energies into their jobs, Eddie and Fran are feeling their energies draining away. They aren't communicating any better than they were, if as well.

One night recently Eddie came home after he'd drunk too much and forced Fran to have sex with him, even though she pleaded with him that she wasn't protected. Actually she was, but it frightened her to think that Eddie really could get her pregnant against her will.

It wasn't the only time he'd abused her. One time he came home from work early and made a scene that scared the children Fran was caring for. He yelled at them to get out of his house and caused them to cry. The children were still upset when the parents came to pick them up. Three families later decided to pull their children out of Fran's day-care operation. That has cost the couple money as well as hurt Fran's reputation. Fran is feeling herself withdraw from Eddie, dreading the end of the day, not knowing what kind of shape he'll be in.

It's been a long time since they've made love spontaneously and passionately. It's been even longer since they've held a serious conversation.

Encountering the Limits of Compatibility

As we look at these three couples in light of our stage theory categories, we can see that each of them is facing a period of disequilibrium due to the limitations of Stage Two marriage. Roles and rules cannot solve some important problems that these couples have experienced. Affection *(storge)* is not a strong enough bond to hold them together through the current stresses.

Allen and Barbara seem more aware of their needs than the other two couples. Even though their life has undergone the biggest change, they seem to be coping the best. Charlie and Donna seem settled into a classic Stage Two marriage. But certain pressures—their relations with their parents, the need for a value structure such as a church, the differences in their attitudes toward work, their unresolved problems about having children—

all these forces seem to be converging at a time when their resources are at a low. As for Eddie and Fran, the dependencies and insecurities of Stage One still rule their life. They've made very few negotiated agreements that can build affection between them. Yet they are beginning to face strains in their relationship that would require the resources of Stage Three—and the prospects for that seem remote indeed.

Pre-Adolescence: Developing the Capacity for Friendship

Do you remember your earliest childhood playmates? You used to spend hours together, creating your own fantasy world where the two of you could live, beyond the reach or even the understanding of the adults who controlled that other world. At some point—and it's always a series of points, isn't it?—you began to confide in each other about your relationship to that adult world. Your conversations no longer were based only on pretend situations. You could actually tell about your parents, your feelings, your experiences. And here was another person, someone your own age, who could understand and would care.

From Playmates to Friendships

These budding friendships, emerging with your playmates, actually started quite early in your childhood. In their early stages, these relationships revolved around "play." The context of the play was a script you were writing as you went along. Each of you acted out the roles, complete with dress-up costumes, props, and sometimes an audience of younger siblings. This type of role playing, which is central to Stage Two, begins to give way to communication about the real world at age six or seven. And the shift continues through ages eight to twelve until, by the early teens, we rarely think of our peers as "playmates." (The fact that this term has acquired a new meaning as a result of the sexual revolution must await the section on Stage Four for further reflection.)

The shift from childhood to pre-adolescence is crucial in our development of the capacity for friendship. In this stage our intellectual and emotional development bestow upon us some vital and powerful resources. These resources will become evident as we trace:
—the move from rules to principles
—the rise of the self in relation to others

71

—the self-preservation motif known as "conformity"
—the crisis of choosing among competing conformities
—the development of elementary self-criticism
—the uses of role models
—the pre-adolescent version of religious values
—the sexual purpose of the "latency period"

From Rules to Principles

One of the events that signals the ending of childhood is the development of a capacity to discover principles to live by rather than to obey specific rules that spell out correct behavior in given situations. The change from rules to principles is a complex learning experience.

In your first few years of life, you quickly found yourself engaged in this rules-to-principles process, without knowing what to call it. Your experience probably went something like this:

You're having a wonderful time sitting in the middle of the floor, pounding a pan with a wooden spoon and enjoying the sense of control that comes from being able to call up loud noises on command. But now here comes little toddler brother or sister, who's also fascinated by the racket. As toddler comes near, you find that your wooden spoon can hit other objects besides the pan, with the even more spectacular effects of bringing forth the toddler's horrified screams.

Then suddenly your control is taken away. An adult grabs the spoon out of your hand, and then, completely unbidden, you feel a smack of pain on your hand, and hear an unsolicited cry coming from your own lips. That's how you learned the rule that you can hit a pan with a spoon but you can't hit little toddler.

Later the rules proliferate: You can't hit little toddler with a truck. Or with a plastic doll. You can't hit little toddler with your hand. Or kick or bite.

Then the rules become more abstract. You can't hit the little girl next door. Or squeeze the new kitty down the street. You can't even hurt anybody's toys. You can't yell at people. And finally, even when it doesn't bother anybody else, you're not allowed to hurt yourself.

The intellectual power of a child is not developed enough in the early years to see a pattern to all these rules. The child is the legalist *ne plus ultra*. Eventually, as the patterns emerge, the need diminishes for a separate rule governing each action. Rules are replaced by principles, which make life immeasurably simpler while putting much heavier responsibility upon the individual to apply principles with careful judgment.

Most children do manage to emerge out of the stage of living by rules into the stage of living by principles. Psychologically speaking, however, many persons remain in the rule stage right through adulthood. These are the persons whose pre-adolescence is primarily a rerun of their childhood. These are also the ones who find Stage Two a comfortable resting place for their love relationships.

Letting Others into My Center

In the pre-adolescent stage young people learn to go beyond an ego-centered view of reality, and to look at the world in interpersonal terms. They can form their own images of themselves while realizing that others view them differently. They also realize that others of their own age are having to form images of themselves. As they compare these self-images with one another, they come to realize the difference between their views of themselves and the views their friends reflect. A major task for pre-adolescents is to pull these differences together, to try to relate their self-image to the images others have.

The tasks usually begin with the significant others in the young person's life—brothers and sisters, parents, close friends. Young people depend on these persons, parents especially, to maintain the sense of identity being built up during pre-adolescence. You may remember being in this stage yourself, and your gradual yet sometimes painful awareness of other people's judgments. You probably felt a deep concern about what other people thought of you.

Pre-adolescence often brings with it a new reliance on interpersonal values, replacing the more self-centered values of childhood. This development reflects the rise of "self-consciousness." What we really mean by this term, however, is the rise of a new consciousness of the self in relation to others. As children we were more conscious of ourselves than we were of others. Most of us can recall at least one childhood experience in which we brought embarrassment to our parents by behaving inappropriately in public. (My parents remember my launching into the '40s hit "Rose O'Day" in the middle of a communion service at church when I was three years old.) "Self-consciousness," or awareness of self in relation to others, is a mark of our emotional maturity, and a necessary stage on the way to personal independence.

The interpersonal is the realm most visible among the leaders and role models that pre-adolescents look to for authority. Qualities such as sincerity, loyalty, courage, genuineness, and self-assurance begin to replace the earlier admiration for external, impersonal qualities reflected in uniform, clear-cut roles, rigid views of right and wrong, and the virtues of strength, success, consistency. The interpersonal values are the ones that sustain relationships and keep alive the attraction between young persons and their role models.

Pre-adolescents tend to take seriously the personal qualities of leaders in the family, school, and church. They look to these social institutions to make certain behavior legitimate or acceptable.

Pre-adolescents do not like to deal with highly specialized relationships. Their religious values tend to be interpersonal. This is the stage at which they continue to see God in terms of power, size, and other impersonal symbols, but they begin to find more understanding in personal qualities: God as Companion, as Friend, Comforter, Counselor, Guide. Pre-adolescents begin to develop religious values based on personal relationships with God and with friends, Bible teachers, and role models in the church.

Without first developing these interpersonal values, pre-adolescents would be unable to move on to form other, higher values that require abstract thinking based on philosophical principles.

Interpersonal values also prepare a pre-adolescent for relationships that can transcend roles. These new values develop out of the experience of viewing myself in relationship to others. They are a necessary step toward enabling me to allow another person into the center of my life. The essence of friendship is the sharing of personal values. Role marriages can be built on a common set of rules and customs, but a friendship marriage cannot exist unless the partners share a common set of basic personal values. The way out of customs and into personal values first begins during pre-adolescence. And a crucial stage in the transition is the much-criticized form of behavior known as conformity.

Conformity: Necessary Step to Independence

The casual observer thinks of pre-adolescence as an age of conformity, for young people in this stage are acutely aware of the judgments and expectations of others. There's much more to it than that. A tension exists between the sense of identity that young people are striving to build and the identities of others. Pre-adolescents are not yet mature enough to live entirely out of their own identities. They haven't had time to pull enough principles together to construct a world view. They're not really mature enough to hold onto an independent set of values that might go against the values of others around them. The constant comparison of one's own norms of behavior with those of parents, siblings, and friends is a preparation for later independence.

Parents often worry that their children will get hurt in this stage of conformity to their peers. They fear their children will reject the values the parents have tried to instill and will adopt the untried values of their peers. Ironically, many parents unintentionally encourage the very conformity they hope to discourage. This happens when they try to rush their children through the age of conformity or to prevent them from even entering it. Either way, the effect is to obstruct the natural process that leads from conformity to independence.

The best thing parents can do for their pre-adolescent children is to be sure they themselves have emerged into a stage of independence. It helps if the parents are not conformists to a peer group of their own. Back when the parents were pre-adolescents themselves, they too struggled to develop a system of values that was distinct from, yet compatible with, the value systems of their friends and their communities. Their memories of their own painful experiences can be of great benefit when talking with their pre-adolescent children about peer pressure.

It is very hard for young persons not to become conformists to a world view if that is what their parents have done. The young people who are most likely to lapse into adopting the values of their peer group are the ones whose parents are uncritical conformists to a set of cultural or religious values.

Pre-adolescents will have a better chance of moving through conformity if their parents have already made their own personal struggle to develop a set of values. These values will be more than mechanistic and predictable expressions of popular ideals. When his or her parents have done more than arbitrarily accept a set of values to which they themselves conform, a young person can develop a strong, independent set of values that can resist peer pressure.

Making Values My Own

It's not easy to make a personal appropriation of a set of values, either as a young person or as a parent. For one thing, there is the pressure of competing or even conflicting conformities. The family tradition offers one set of values. The school environment may offer others. The church may have another, and the general culture still another. Small wonder that pre-adolescent fantasies about the future offer various means of escape from the so-called real world. Young people are often caught in a tug-of-war. They may have a great deal of difficulty meeting the varieties of expectations. They have to learn to tolerate and live with the different evaluations of their behavior that are made by people in so many differing groups. In spite of the difficulties, however, young people usually find a way to synthesize these different expectations and judgments. In their search, they generally try several solutions before settling on a set of personal values.

Segmentation. One solution pre-adolescents try is to segment or compartmentalize life. When they are with their parents, they behave as their parents expect them to. When they are with their peers, they do as their peers expect. The effect is to cut life into pieces, and to live out of compartments. Parents can play a crucial role in helping resolve this dilemma. They can make it easier for their pre-adolescent children by trying to understand the various points of view that young people are being pressured to live by. The parents may recall the kinds of pressures that peers applied in their own pre-adolescent periods. If they are honest, parents will realize how they continue as adults to face conflicting sets of values—at home, at work, at church, with various groups of friends. Sensitive and understanding parents can keep from becoming just one more compartment in a child's life. If they are understanding of the conflicting pressures, their child is more likely to form a trusting relationship with them. Together they can discuss the ways to avoid segmentation as a way of coping with value conflicts.

Pyramiding. The second response that pre-adolescents tend to use in coping with the different sets of expectations is to arrange the pressure groups in a hierarchy. In this way, the young person decides which of the various groups are the most important, which are the least important, and which fall somewhere in between. While the groups are all present simultaneously, some offer more important help than others. For example, a young person may choose the peers' values as the most important and the parents' second, the church's third, and the school's fourth. The result is that their behavior is influenced by all of these pressures but not in equal measure. Therefore, none of the sets of values will offer a final and exclusive claim on the young person's life.

This is probably the healthier of the two responses at this stage in the young person's life, the one that offers more resources for a more mature set of values in the future. The process for arranging priorities can be excruciating. It demands more honesty and consistency than does segmentation. Pre-adolescents can expect to fail more often because their goals are higher. Parents can be more forgiving and more encouraging, knowing that their children will accept some parental values and reject others but also knowing that they will behave in front of their parents the same way they do with their peers.

Predicting Consequences of My Actions

Pre-adolescence is the stage where young people can begin to develop the ability to think about their own thinking processes and to evaluate their evaluation processes. They are able to try to imagine how their behavior looks to their parents or to school officials or the church. By thinking about their own thought processes, they are able to develop a certain inner logic and a certain predictability about the reactions people have to their behavior. Therefore, they are able to imagine some hypothetical possibilities of the consequences of actions they might take. They can understand how these actions are likely to affect other people.

At this stage the young person's beliefs and values still come largely from significant others, primarily the parents, with the peer group consensus on the ascendancy. These beliefs received from parents may be deeply felt and deeply held. They may characterize the young person's behavior. Even so, the authority for these values comes primarily from the respect that the child has developed for those who have offered these values. They haven't been thought out. They haven't been appropriated for their own sake. They seem self-evident. They seem to be those values that work best for the people whom they respect the most. Thus the role model enters the picture.

Role models who exhibit certain types of behavior tend to have a strong impact on young people in this stage. Pre-adolescents have not yet made a personal inventory, have not yet made evaluations for themselves, of the possibilities for life. They are not particularly reflective, philosophical, or interested in comparing abstract lifestyles. Instead, they watch how these various lifestyles are exhibited by people who have committed themselves to them.

Pre-adolescents can be very observant of what is approved and what is frowned on by various social institutions. The leaders they tend to follow the most, and the institutions they tend to respect the most, are those that look the part. They look to leaders who express in their own lifestyle, their own mannerisms, and their own behavior and speech what is conventionally expected of them. Pre-adolescents don't particularly admire leaders who step out of character: adults who try to be buddies, peers who try to act too grown-up, representatives of various groups who try to be too individualistic. This is the stage in which certain teachers, soldiers, entertainers, rock stars, all exert a particular influence on the young.

Trust is also placed in a leader who has the approval of a valued institution. Schools affect the young person in this stage by their attitudes toward certain leadership roles within the institution—cheerleaders, football players, straight-A students, or musicians. If a school offers citations and awards to students for certain behavior, then these winners are viewed as role models. Such institutions can either help or hinder pre-adolescents. Leaders whose lifestyle is consistent with the values they profess can help by giving their approval and encouragement to young people who are struggling to develop personal values rather than to those who are slavishly imitating the current fads.

For the most part, young people in this stage enjoy being a part of small groups because the purpose of small groups is to furnish face-to-face relationships. The groups naturally tend to be small, and young persons look for those individuals with whom they have rapport in many different areas of life. The group activities that lead to loving relationships are different from the groups whose primary aim is to promote teamwork, competitive drive, or short-term success. Athletic teams, church youth groups, music groups and other special interest organizations have other priorities than that of developing relational values. Sometimes young people do manage to turn these group activities to their own advantage. The very fact that these groups provide opportunities for communication among individuals means that some relational activity will take place. But until very recently most pre-adolescents have had to develop their own institutions for developing close relationships. The all-night slumber party and the no-girls-allowed gang are traditional examples.

Same-Sex Groups: Prerequisite to Opposite-Sex Intimacy

Pre-adolescent male groups and female groups play an important role in a young person's development. In these groups, young boys learn some important new dimensions of being male. Young girls learn how it feels to live without worrying about the presence of boys. The atmosphere is more relaxed and conducive to taking risks and exploring possibilities. When a pre-adolescent takes part in a same-sex group, he or she can take the first steps out of expected roles. When girls are by themselves, they find it easier to slip out of the sugar-and-spice-and-everything-nice roles, just as boys-only groups are freer to shed the snakes-snails-puppy-dog-tails expectations. In a same-sex group, a wide variety of emotions and activities can occur. Girls can play rough sports, test their stamina, talk about boys, discuss deep topics, and try any number of other activities that might falter under the inhibiting pressures of being Daddy's little girl and Bubba's kid sister. Boys can camp out, cook, wash and repair their clothes, make their beds, get scared at night, talk about girls, and find out about a whole range of natural activities not expected of the little man of the house, the kid brother. To discover the full range of one's own gender is the challenge of pre-adolescence.

The time will come soon enough when boys and girls find it safe to be around persons of the opposite sex. The arrival of puberty provides the physiological force to set in motion the relational change. But the pre-adolescent period of sexual latency is just as important as adolescence, though not as visibly dramatic.

Philia: Brotherly Love Is for Sisters, Too

In this period a new style of loving became possible. This new style can be characterized by the Greek word *philia*, translated as "friendship" or "brotherly love." In this period, friendship now becomes exalted to a higher level than ever before. Friendship was the new relationship based on the presupposition of the full equality of all humanity—as Paul the apostle put it, of Jew and Gentile, of male and female, slave and free. All are one. All are brothers and sisters.

Brotherly love transcended love based on rules or roles. In the legalistic framework, love was strictly controlled. But the new emphasis on *philia* or brotherly love came to be characterized by a moral and spiritual communion that broke across the barriers between slavery and freedom, between the sexes, between cultures. Love could be expressed with the mind and the will. It could enable people to enjoy one another contemplatively and devotedly. Once *philia* was discovered, it put *eros* and *storge* into a new context. For a time *eros* was renounced and condemned. For a time the ethics of *storge*, based on rules, rewards and punishments, were forced into the background.

How Brotherly Love Transformed Sexual Love

Later, as the way of life characterized by brotherly love became more stable, there was an attempt to go beyond the denial of *eros*. There was an attempt to integrate *eros* into brotherly love. The ideal shifted from the separation of the sexes in monasteries to a new ideal in which a man and a woman could desire each other, marry, and be friends. After the centuries in which *philia* or brotherly love was expressed by the segregation of the sexes in the monasteries, the idea began to emerge that a person could marry one's best friend. Marriage was not simply based on biological necessity, on *eros*. Nor was marriage based on *storge*, on community customs or rules. It could be based on the spiritual values which the two persons already shared as members of the human family.

The Current State of Friendship Marriage

Not every couple who has the potential to do so will make the transition from role marriage to friendship marriage. The forces that keep a relationship from moving out of Stage Two are quite powerful. Even so, Stage Three exerts an even stronger attraction to those who become aware of its possibilities. Couples can loosen the hold of role-playing on their marriage by working together through the dynamics that produce friendship. Those who add the higher, more difficult ideal of friendship marriage do so by gradually developing a set of common values and an enjoyment of common activities. No couple arrives at the friendship stage on their wedding day. Even those who enter marriage with a wide range of common values find that they must work to translate the values into specific activities. And those who enjoy a lot of common activities come to realize that, unless the activities lead to better communication and understanding, they can be barriers to intimacy rather than bridges.

In many stable, happy Stage Two marriages, each partner's best friend is someone else, someone of the same sex. In these marriages, the partners recapitulate the pre-adolescent stage of friendship. They do not cross the threshold into opposite-sex friendship.

The most combustible mixture of all is the marriage in which one partner (or both) have a best friend of the opposite sex outside a role marriage. Friendship has the power to transform roles. But a marriage based on roles is usually a poor match for an opposite-sex friendship.

As your two personalities mature, and as the two of you tap into higher spiritual and social values, the potential for living out the deepest dimensions of friendship will exert an almost irresistible upward pull on your relationship. Never again can you be satisfied with hierarchical and legalistic forms of love, played by rules and expressed in roles.

81

The impact of friendship marriage in our society is incalculable. Its creative overflow has empowered virtually every institution we value.

The modern church is inconceivable without the voluntary support, both financial and moral, of persons who live conventional married lives. The public and private schools also draw their most loyal constituencies from the Stage Three consciousness. So do the political parties, relief agencies, and the myriad movements for reform.

Strong family unity, based not on rigid roles but on a mutual commitment, has been assumed until only recently by the government, the military, and the large corporations. Seldom in history has there been a larger unilateral transfer of power and willing sacrifice than from the conventional nuclear family to the larger institutions of our culture.

Today, however, the many pressures that have been drawing upon the friendship marriage have reached a limit. The friendship marriage is gasping for breath. We are in desperate need of receiving some return on our investment. Somewhere the dependent institutions must find the resources to pay the dividends. Unless that happens, we shall soon see every public institution we value begin to stagger and stumble, until in their helpless paralysis they destroy the very source of their life.

In response to the almost overwhelming pressures placed on it by our larger institutions, the institution of marriage has emerged in a new form, with new resources, potentialities, and satisfactions.

Marriage today is attempting to meet the deepest personal needs of individuals and also to respond to the most profound challenges of cultural revolution and technological complexity. Tracing these crucial developments in our ways of loving and measuring their impact on the problems we are attempting to solve will be the focus of the next chapter on the Stage Four marriage—and the unique type of "divorce" that accompanies it.

Sharing Your Values: Deepening the Friendship Marriage

On the pages that follow are some areas of discussion that can help you to "raise consciousness" into Stage Three areas of your marriage that remain in Stage Two. The two of you can share your responses with each other.

1. Who were your closest friends during the ages of eight to twelve (third to sixth grades)? Did you participate in all-boys or all-girls groups, such as Scouts or church youth groups, during this time? Did you have any friendships with the opposite sex during this time?

2. What activities do you remember your parents enjoying together? What personality traits did they have in common, as you recall? As a child, what activities did you enjoy most with each parent?

3. In comparing your backgrounds, which of these factors do you have most in common, and which offer the biggest contrast:
—religious values
—economic status
—educational attainments
—career preparation
—attitudes about rearing children

4. Which of the following areas offer you the most and the least compatibility:
—church involvement
—expressing feelings clearly
—money-spending habits
—sexual enjoyment
—job or career satisfaction
—attitudes toward the future

5. A sense of obligation. Duty. Guilt. If these three motivations were to disappear from your life, how would your marriage be different? Which differences are threatening, and which are compelling to you?

6. What projects do you enjoy working on together? When you get a babysitter, where do you usually go? Is this a place you'd go if you didn't have to consider your spouse's interest? How do you usually spend Sunday mornings? Friday nights? Saturday afternoons? Do you feel your life together gets in ruts, or do you feel the balance is about right?

7. How do you compare the friendship element in your marriage with the marriages of your friends? Who among your married friends seem to have a spouse for a best friend?

8. What experiences in your marriage would you say have been examples of courage? What are some examples of personal sacrifices each of you has made in behalf of your relationship?

How do you feel about the sacrifices your spouse has mentioned?

9. Who are your three or four best friends outside your marriage? What do you enjoy most about each of these friends? Not counting brothers or sisters, do you have any friends of the opposite sex? What do you enjoy most about them? How does your spouse feel about your friends of the same sex? Your friends of the opposite sex?

10. In what ways has your relationship developed toward friendship since the early days? What aspects of friendship have you lost as time has passed? What are the qualities of your marriage that have continued since the beginning?

Selected Reading for Background and Discussion

Stage Three

**The Rise of Spiritual Discipline
and Relationships Based on Shared Values**

Dietrich Bonhoeffer, *Life Together*
Elizabeth O'Connor, *Gifts and Creativity*
Floyd and Harriett Thatcher, *Long-Term Marriage*
Harold and Carole Straughn, *Through the Bible with Those Who Were There*
Emil Brunner, *Our Faith*
Michael Novak, *Ascent of the Mountain, Flight of the Dove*
C. S. Lewis, *Mere Christianity*
J. B. Phillips, *New Testament Christianity*
Abraham Heschel, *The Prophets: An Introduction*
Helen Waddell, *The Desert Fathers*
Roland Bainton, *Here I Stand: A Life of Martin Luther*

Stage Four: *Dikaiosune,* Love as a Declaration of Independence

The Adolescent Period of a Relationship

Down by the salley gardens
      my love and I did meet;
She passed the salley gardens
      with little snow-white feet.
She bid me take love easy,
      as the leaves grown on the tree;
But I, being young and foolish,
      with her did not agree.
      —William Butler Yeats, *Down by the Salley Gardens*[6]

Is the price of living with another person
always so steep? Do you always have to
give up a part of yourself that you need?
Is it going to be like this forever
wanting what you want but not being able to have it?
Too many relationships are based on such childish,
unrealistic ideas of possessing each other
that is is difficult to grow and develop as an individual
without hurting the other partner.
      —David Viscott, *How to Live with Another Person*[7]

Nothing is more false than to say to somebody:
since I love you and you love me,
I don't need to get justice from you,
or you from me. . . .
It is said by tyrannical rulers to their subjects
and by tyrannical parents to their children. . . .
Often the love which supposedly transcends justice
is nothing more than an emotional outburst
of self-surrender, alternating with
emotional outbursts of hostility.
  —Paul Tillich, *Love, Power and Justice*[8]

Who decides when a relationship is officially over? In the last generation we bestowed the right and responsibility of decision upon the individual alone. Not even the state, which has the power to declare a marriage officially started, can oppose the wishes of a partner to dissolve a relationship, particularly in parts of the country where "no-fault" divorce law prevails.

Here is a far more anguishing question: How does an individual arrive at the decision to sever the relationship? The end of a marriage is a complex event to measure, far more so than even the end of an individual's life. Yet questions about medical or clinical death are a more familiar subject than the death of a relationship. The news media regularly chronicle the crisis of family members who are divided over how long to continue extraordinary measures to support the ebbing, unconscious, or excruciatingly painful life of a loved one. And the popular press for years has been fascinated with the theme of "hopeless cases" who defied medical prognoses and recovered. (Not to mention the fictional genre of gothic horror tales about people given up for dead who escaped from the grave.)

The tragedy is, most individuals have virtually no formal training for judging the health or the life expectancy of their own relationship when it enters one of its inevitable periods of disequilibrium. Today a person too often has nowhere to turn for perspective. Usually we simply wait until the problems are so overwhelming that we become convinced the relationship cannot possibly survive. A kind of popular folk-wisdom has arisen in the absence of solid evidence. According to this folklore, you know your marriage is in serious trouble when:

—You no longer feel the same way about each other that you did when you first fell in love.

—You no longer enjoy doing the same things together.

—Your outside interests seem to be taking you in opposite directions.

—Your temperaments show no signs of becoming more compatible.

—Your values and attitudes have changed so much that the reasons you got married in the first place no longer apply.

—It's obvious your spouse isn't going to change, even though you've felt for a long time those changes would have to come.

—Your personal growth is more important to you than ever before, yet your marriage is a hindrance, not a help.

—The children no longer depend on you the way they used to.

Almost any one of the above situations would prove threatening to brittle relationships. Marriages that involve violent patterns of physical and mental abuse, and those affected by the self-inflicted violence of alcohol or drugs, fall into the category of dependencies, as we have outlined in earlier chapters. These dependency marriages often collapse of their own weight, without much help from outside forces. For the majority of marriages, however, a period of uncertainty, change, or upheaval too often is taken as a sign that the relationship is headed for the rocks. From the perspective of stage theory, we are learning to look beyond the mere fact of disequilibrium. We are learning to look ahead to the new, more deeply satisfying periods of equilibrium that almost certainly will follow.

Divorce and the Search for Personal Fulfillment

We are coming to see more and more that relationships appear to be dying when in reality they are preparing to pass into a new stage of life. The transition feels like death, if only because it doesn't feel like any experience of life that we know about so far.

Divorce has often become the twentieth-century rite of passage into a new stage of consciousness. Marriage in our time has become the principal casualty of individual growth and the search for identity. This is a fairly new function for divorce to play. Historical perspective helps us to see that what we may assume to

21st Cent. too!

be a universal phenomenon is a recent and, probably, temporary phenomenon. Divorce in earlier civilizations had little or nothing to do with personal growth or incompatibility. Three thousand years ago a man might divorce his wife for failure to provide a son and heir. (Scarcely anyone felt there was much reason for a woman to divorce a man under that system.) In the last few centuries, as medical progress has extended the life span, divorce has taken on a duty that death used to perform in terminating marriages, both good and bad. Even a generation or two ago, early death came to women through childbirth and to men through poor nutrition and harsh working conditions. It seems that in our time marriage has overcome its age-old enemies, only to encounter a uniquely modern apparent threat: the emergence of individual freedom as a primary goal of life.

Marriage and personal growth are often viewed in conventional circles today as potential competitors. Many supposed defenders of marriage have decried the trends in our society toward personal development as inherently selfish forces that corrode relationships. Their voices were added to those who accused marriage and family of complicity with the intractable oppressive forces of the past. Both the defenders and the opponents of marriage seemingly have lined up on the same side of the issue: They both say you can't have personal freedom and lifelong marriage. Choose one or the other. The assumption is so pervasive that virtually all the cultural trends support it. One way to see the assumption at work is to look again at the list of "folklore ideas" found earlier in this chapter.

New evidence is being discovered, however, which indicates that marriage is actually a most potent force in behalf of personal growth. Many who have left a marriage in pursuit of individual freedom report that they have failed to find it, while many who have experienced the evolution of their marriage through the stages we have depicted so far are discovering new levels of liberation. These couples are being swept into a whole range of possibilities for personal development that are staggering in their impact.

In virtually every complex and satisfying marriage, the discoveries seem to emerge only after a period of prolonged crisis in the relationship. In too many cases, tragically, the labor pains of the crisis are so frightening that a couple is led to divorce before the process can give birth to the new stage.

88

The Third Divorce: The Need to Be Independent

The quest for personal freedom and growth is an inevitable part of any healthy marriage. In a Stage One dependency relationship, however, personal freedom threatens the very foundations. It implies that this other person might not always be there to meet my needs. In a Stage Two role marriage, personal freedom appears to break the rules, to erode the sense of obligation, to put self ahead of other. Even in a Stage Three friendship marriage, independence often appears to undermine the sense of sharing that is at the heart of conventional love in our time.

The truth is that virtually every friendship marriage sooner or later is going to confront a major challenge by the force of personal freedom. The quest for individual identity and self-discovery, like all uninvited forces from the future, threatens the satisfying sense of common goals and values so painstakingly developed in Stage Three. The first response is to dismiss the signals that all is not well. As the needs become more insistent, and the signals more persistent, a couple may eventually try to deal with them, but on their own terms. The new needs cannot be met under existing conditions, however, for they bring their own, non-negotiable terms. Faced with a force of such power, many couples mistakenly interpret their needs for personal growth as a sign that their marriage cannot survive. One partner or the other may mistake the signals as an indication that some other person can fill the need. As a result, a new relationship with an outsider may be conceived and born, when the need was actually for a new and more mature level of intimacy with each other.

moving in ministry

Every couple will, as we have said, experience in different ways the rise of personal independence. One crucial factor is the impact of our adolescent experience on our adult relationships. Another decisive force is the rise of individual liberty in the last few centuries and its impact upon the cultural environment in which our own personal quests occur.

As we begin our reflection together on these two influences, it's time to look in once again on the three composite couples whose lives reflect some typical ways of coping with "the third divorce."

Allen and Barbara. It happened to them when their daughter was old enough to go to school. Barbara, instead of working on other people's political campaigns, decided she wanted to run for the local school board. It would demand her time, money, and organizational ability, plus the energy to speak at nights, sit at coffees, and plan media campaigns. Her goal was to oust an incumbent who was profiting indirectly from school construction contracting. She knew it could be a dirty campaign. The incumbent felt nothing but contempt for her knowledge and experience.

Allen now finds himself being introduced by his friends as "her lovely husband, Allen." Eventually it began to sting, though he brushed it off at first, for he was a liberated man. Most of all he was proud of Barbara and believed in her cause. Even so, nights at home followed the days at home. He fixed her meals and put their daughter to bed. He showed up at the right places, stayed away from others. Now Allen was feeling strangely pressured by roles. Not since early marriage had he felt so hemmed in by roles and rules. Some days he felt sick and depressed. Yet he couldn't admit his resentment to himself. He felt guilty and ashamed of his resentment. He began to experience a drop in creativity and productivity at the very time Barbara needed him most. He felt like a failure. Barbara had helped him; now it was Allen's turn, and he was letting her down.

In time, Allen found himself attracted to a lovely young girl who admired his painting. With this soft, communicative, erotic, open, available young woman he felt an instant mutual attraction. And suddenly, a tailspin. Allen felt he was falling in love. He tried to convince himself it was infatuation or even just loneliness. But his head was full of her. There was nothing stopping them from her side. She understood, she said, and could supply the intimacy and support he needed. She would be glad to oblige, because Allen was by far one of the most fascinating older men she'd ever met. She was adventuresome enough to give him just the amount of encouragement to draw him nearer. But not too much so as to scare him away. Allen began losing his health. At times he thought he was going crazy. He wondered what was happening, as fever, lack of sleep, lack of appetite wracked him.

And yet—what was it that kept him at the edge of the abyss, but not over it? Something was doing it. It wasn't the usual pricks of conscience or duty or guilt. It was something he'd never felt before. He felt a subterranean, churning, turning, sea change. The ocean floor of his being was rising up, engulfing the surface and thrusting it into the deep. All he could do was behold in amazement as this power from within seized control of his life in crisis and pointed across the abyss to what was being prepared for him. What he saw was a new relationship, a new intimacy, with a new woman. The mystery lover, it turned out, was Barbara. Now she was renewed as a person, a community leader in her own right, on her own terms, a victor, in behalf of quality education and the whole child, over the forces of "business as usual" and callous greed. Never had she appeared more radiant. Never was he more deeply, passionately, committedly in love with her. It was as though death itself had died, and in its place had emerged the rebirth of all for which he and she had invested their lives. Now it had returned to them immeasurably richer.

As for the soft, young, open beauty, she too has become her own person, believing in herself and in her right to a deep intimacy instead of the temporary, desperate contacts she had experienced one after the other. She and Allen can openly say to each other that they love each other. And they can tell others also. It is a public, growing expression of love that can grow alongside his marriage and her singleness, without threatening to dissolve the relationships of either one. This is their commitment to each other: that they respond to each other as caring friends, as intimate confidantes, as spiritual brother and sister. As part of their faithfulness they have taken a vow of sexual celibacy with each other, so that their close friendship may flourish and so that Allen and Barbara's marriage will be affirmed and encouraged. And the young woman's singleness is hers to share with another if she pleases.

Charlie and Donna. No one, least of all Charlie, knows why his insurance agency failed. The downturn in the economy, the increase of group policies, the intrusion of so many new companies into Charlie's territory, the number of highly trained and aggressive agents now in competition with him—all could have contributed to the failure.

It was quite a blow when Charlie had to join a larger, more established traditional firm, in the lower rungs of the company, with less base salary and little room for personal initiative to move up or out. At thirty-five, Charlie is starting over—and feeling trapped.

Donna, meanwhile, is the regional manager for over a dozen Dairy Queen stores, a tribute in part to her dogged hard work and in part to the convenient financing arranged through her father's contacts with local banks. Charlie has chosen some new territories in outlying cities, in hopes, he tells Donna, of outworking the agents who prefer staying closer to home. In reality, the nights spent away from home provide a much-needed release from the treadmill race he and Donna have been running for years—a race Donna appears to be winning decisively.

Charlie never intended to get into a breadwinning contest with his wife, and it certainly never occurred to him that once the contest began that he might even lose it. If he'd even imagined such an outcome back years ago when Donna started taking orders over the counter at that first store. . . . But there are other women in other towns who aren't nearly so threatening, and his feelings of impotence, emotional and sexual, are beginning to recede, as long as he's away from home.

Donna finds it a relief to be able to work hard all day, make it to the front door, fix herself a simple supper, take a long relaxing soak, and tumble into a long, calm renewing sleep.

Every one of those new stores has been like a child to her—demanding every ounce of her energy yet rewarding her with a sense of accomplishment and public recognition. It was a shock to her when Charlie had to change jobs, but it didn't change her mind about him. She still loved him even though she was making more money this year than he was. She couldn't relate to him, though, when he'd get in his unpredictable and brooding moods. Better for her that he stayed away when he was feeling that way. You couldn't talk to him even when he was home.

There was a compartment in her mind where she learned to keep her thoughts about his whereabouts on his nights away from home, where she kept her thoughts safely locked away from even her own view.

Eddie and Fran. It came to a climax the night Eddie came home drunk and kept Fran frightened all night long with his violent threats and his uncontrolled, sobbing self-deprecation. The next morning Fran had to be ready to turn her house into a day-care center, just as though nothing had happened. Eddie slept through most of the day. When he awoke late in the afternoon, he discovered that all his clothes and portable belongings were packed in boxes and stacked outside on the porch. Instead of arguing or fighting, Eddie took a couple of suitcases and left the house.

After a few hours of driving around town, Eddie began to realize that the many people he and Fran had taken care of in earlier times were not exactly lining up to take him in. So Eddie spent the next several nights in a motel.

After several weeks of being away, Eddie returned home. He' made it a point not to drink too much this time. He and Fran sat down and told each other how much they'd missed each other. They spent the night in each other's arms.

Eddie had been back home only a few weeks when the doctor confirmed what Fran had come to dread. Fran was pregnant, and at the worst possible time. There was no way she could bring a child into the world she inhabits. For several days it was all Fran could do to hold herself together. Then the cloud of depression suddenly lifted. Fran began to feel the return of her sense of self-confidence and resolve.

Almost too quickly, Eddie thought. Something was not quite right about Fran's turnabout. Eddie got more and more suspicious, and finally confronted her.

He was right. Fran had made her decision to get an abortion. Furious, confused, helpless, and at the edge of his breaking point, Eddie ordered Fran not to do it. He threatened to kill her. He pleaded and screamed at her. He smashed his fist through the wall and began to cry uncontrollably.

But Fran had made up her mind. For the first time in years she felt she was actually in control of some aspect of her life.

When Friendship Marriages Falter

Once again these three couples are heading into periods of disequilibrium. In various ways they are discovering how friendship has its limits. The common values they share appear to be disintegrating. The individual needs, desires, and choices seem to be opposed to a warm and comfortable relationship. Even more disturbing, each of the relationships feels out of control, unresponsive to the attempts of any of the partners to keep the friendship elements alive.

Along with these similarities, each relationship is coping in distinctively different ways.

In Allen and Barbara's case, she is pursuing her personal achievements in politics by building on the foundation of her relationship to Allen. She does not threaten Allen, since he does not mind living in her shadow or reversing their familiar roles. His problem is with the tactical retreat he has to make back into Stage Two to accommodate her schedule. He struggles with the feelings of regression brought on by the new role he must play. The combination of necessary change and fearful reluctance, of acceleration combined with braking, led to a prolonged depression.

Allen's crisis is not role-reversal, however; it's self-image. He has a hard time accepting a picture of himself as a sacrifical martyr, or as a patronizing benefactor, or as a temporary hired hand. So he is vulnerable to an appeal to his artistic nature, which he is having to suppress for the time being. The beautiful young admirer of his painting ability is able to enter quickly into his life.

Even so, a powerful force is at work in Allen's life that helps him stop short of allowing a "supplementary" relationship to develop. Allen knows himself well enough to see that she is not the answer to his problems; he is. The depth of this self-knowledge proves strong enough to help carry Allen and Barbara's marriage across the threshold into Stage Four.

Charlie and Donna's plight shows what happens when a couple still struggling to make it from Stage Two to Stage Three face a challenge from Stage Four. Charlie's role in business defines his identity. If he loses his job he loses his self-worth. So low is his self-esteem after the job fiasco that the new job can appear to him only as somebody's opportunistic attempt to exploit him. Imperceptibly he begins to resent those who are above him instead of being challenged by them as he had always done before.

Donna's successes only rub in Charlie's setbacks. Slowly their comfortable roles have reverted to competitive power plays. In a relationship, tragically for them, nobody wins if anybody loses. The relationship can never exceed the .500 mark if one partner is winning and the other is losing.

Charlie's response is to compartmentalize for the sake of safety. Like a sinking ship taking water, he tries to seal off some compartments of his mind. He shuts off his sexual feelings from Donna. He shuts off his emotional and intellectual needs from his

94

out-of-town contacts. Sex, of course, is too powerful a force to be channeled wherever the will commands it to go. Its intention is always to break down barriers between the mind, will, and feelings, and—if left to itself—to create intimate communion out of physical sensations.

Donna is also caught in some competitiveness and some compartmentalizing of her own. She, too, draws a great deal of self-esteem from her achievements, even when (especially when?) they are made at Charlie's expense. Now that their roles are reversed, and she's making more money than he is, the release of her newfound energy is poured back into her job, not into the relationship.

Donna would tell you that she's willing to be more open with Charlie but that he's too brittle. But there's more to it than that. She can't share her feelings with him because she can't admit them to herself. She can't accept how important her job is for propping up her self-esteem. She can't confide her fear of loss, her terror at sensing that what she does defines who she is.

Charlie and Donna haven't yet found the common values upon which to build a marriage dedicated to personal growth. As a result, they have settled on a chilling way to cope: saving the marriage by sacrificing intimacy.

It seems that Eddie and Fran still are trapped by their dependencies. Few opportunities for personal growth have yet arisen from their relationship. Love is still being viewed as a sacrifice, not as a power to draw from. Other people have depended on Eddie and Fran, but these friends are unable to return the love they have received. Freeloaders who take more than they give dominate Eddie and Fran. Even Eddie's alcohol and Fran's child care center continue to demand more and more while delivering less and less.

These two appealing yet pitiable people could use a few rules and a few well-defined roles. They view rules and roles as beneath them, even though life gets tedious when they have to get up each morning to re-invent and redefine their relationship before they can get on with the day. Their fear of commitment is taking more and more energy to maintain.

Eddie and Fran still find it easier to give to others than to receive for themselves. That tends to block what little giving they offer each other. Because of their lack of experience in the give-

and-take of deep sharing, they tend to overreact and overcompensate. Fran throws Eddie out. Eddie responds with further self-directed violence, no more able to stand his ground and negotiate his grievances than Fran is. Yet he can't exist out in the world on his own. One can only imagine the effect on Eddie's self-esteem as he comes back home. His return is no better negotiated than was his leaving. With no commitment, no security, no sharing, the only communication channel they have left is sex. And what a statement they've now made!

An unplanned pregnancy. Yet there was nothing free or spontaneous about the grim, sullen, hostile emotions that raged back and forth unspoken between them. It could have been a time for celebrating their commitment to bring a child into the world and to rear a mature adult together. But the commitment is not there.

Fran wants to destroy the growing sign of their intimacy before it can make any more of an impact than it already has. Eddie's against the abortion, but he's in no shape to assume any responsibility. His powerful, conflicting feelings are canceling each other out, leaving him ready to commit violence to protest his helplessness. And Fran, feeling independent for perhaps the first time in her life, will have to destroy in order for it to survive.

The "Third Divorce":
Crisis in the American Friendship Marriage

It is virtually impossible to overestimate the impact of friendship marriage on our society. Democratic forms of government, corporate enterprise, volunteer activism all are inconceivable without the foundation provided by the marriage style that emphasizes the sharing of basic values.

Yet friendship marriage is precisely the style that is showing the greatest increase in breakdown in our society. (Dependency marriages have always been unstable, while role marriages seemingly are less affected by divorce than those that reach Stage Three.)

How are we to account for this apparent imperiling, and what is the likely outcome to these institutions when their foundations crumble?

If history is any guide, the decline of marriage based on shared values generally produces a retreat into an earlier stage of

96

marriage. Such a shift usually has created subterranean instability and pressure, which results in tremors and violent quakes to the ground above. Such cultural retreats have occurred again and again, arguing against any facile theory of continuous progress in society.

There have been times in our history, however, when threats to conventional marriage styles have led to new forms of relationships with positive consequences for society as a whole.

Our own time seems to offer abundant examples of both trends. We see a retreat to and renewal of traditional values, as political and religious conservatism rises to power at every level. Simultaneously, we witness today more political power and public acceptance of unconventional sexual behavior than at any time in American history. (The history of Europe, the Roman Empire, classical Greece, and ancient Egypt are, however, a different matter.)

It is impossible to predict which movement will push the country the farthest. Yet some signs are visible that give us reason to hope that marriage will not lapse back into the narrowness and rigidity that generations fought so hard to overcome. Nor is the evidence so conclusive that the conventional ideal of one man and one woman, friends for life, is doomed to burial by an avalanche of experiments in single parent, serial, contractual, homosexual, triadic, "open," or polygamous styles. These surface manifestations of ferment and turmoil may be hiding rather than revealing the most significant changes happening to marriages in our time.

One thing is conclusive nevertheless: Conventional friendship marriages are beginning to metamorphose into something new. And this new form does resemble in important ways the experimental styles just mentioned. While a thoroughly clear picture of what is happening is not yet available to us, certain signs already can account for the present decline in the conventional marriage ideal.

Why Friendship Marriage Is Declining

Certain inherent weaknesses in friendship marriage begin to show up when we reflect on its nature from the perspective of stage development theory. The key insight is that friendship mar-

97

riage draws its resources from the pre-adolescent stage of the two partners' personality development and from the stage of historical development in which the human race experienced a kind of "cultural pre-adolescence." In earlier chapters we've described the positive side of these developments, comparing them favorably to the stages that had gone before. Now it is time to analyze them from the perspective of Stage Four. Let us understand the new forces that are unleashed during the adolescent stage of personality development and that are bequeathed to us from the period of human history that exhibits a "cultural adolescence."

1. *Friendship marriage is rooted in same-sex relationships.* The personality resources for friendships first develop among pre-adolescents of the same sex. Friendship marriages usually carry over many of the patterns which the two partners learned back in their pre-puberty associations. For millions of couples, their ways of communicating, of expressing feelings, of asserting themselves, were discovered in their very early same-sex friendships, and have changed very little in the ensuing years. One result is that nonsexual communication carries over only with great difficulty into sexual activity. Couples with lingering pre-adolescent communications techniques find it hard to move smoothly from practical concerns to personal and emotional expressions of feeling, to sexual arousal, to sexual communication, to physical intimacy, to intercourse—and back through the process to the outside world. The intellectual and physiological capacity to move freely through this process does not even begin until well along in adolescence. If we fail to develop these capacities, available to us since adolescence, our sexuality throughout life tends to be an erratic, unstable colloidal suspension of innocence and guilt, pleasure and performance, intimacy and alienation.

2. *Friendship marriage emphasizes the universal over the unique.* The ideals of universal human community, of universal truth, and the brotherhood and sisterhood of humanity, are the forebears of friendship marriage. Not all the effects of this heritage have proved beneficial. There has been a tendency, for example, to stress the universal attributes of all marriages to the downgrading of the distinctive aspects that make each relationship unique.

98

As long as our problems are like those found in every marriage, we are usually safe in trying to find out how others have resolved the difficulties and in following their examples. It is a commonplace of conventional therapy today to reassure an anxious seeker that "you are not alone in your problem. You are not the only one." The relief that follows this discovery is often all the therapy that is needed. Obviously, if all couples experience the same problems, and if the solution to the problems works the same way for all, it goes a lot easier for marriage counselors to prescribe the same techniques to all. However, when we start trying to surface the unique aspects of any relationship, we generally cross into uncharted territory.

It was a profound insight into our tendency to overemphasize universal values which led Leo Tolstoy to observe that "happy families are all alike; every unhappy family is unhappy in its own way." Happy families are those whose lives fit the conventional prescriptions; those who do not fit the conventions are distressed by their differences, and are made to feel outside the circle, alienated, and unique.

3. *Conflicts cannot always be resolved by appeal to basic principles.* The very strength of friendship marriage often proves to be its undoing. The couple enters the relationship confident that the basic values they share can help them resolve their conflicts. The fact that most of the time their shared values do serve them well only intensifies the anguish and frustration when the principles don't seem to work.

What should a couple do when their basic values appear to let them down? The first inclination is to give the values another chance. After all, a universal principle is supposed to work in all situations. When it does not appear to be doing so, that cannot be the fault of the principles, we say to ourselves; it must be you—or I—who is at fault.

Sometimes, however, the problem persists. Nothing the two of us share, nothing either of us knows, is enough to resolve the problem. The longer the problem continues, the more the two of us begin to blame each other, and the more desperately we cling to the principles we have learned to trust over the years.

Into virtually every relationship comes a crisis which will not go away, no matter how fervently the partners trust the beliefs they hold. For many couples, the crisis is resolved when they reaffirm their belief in their value system. They trust that things somehow will work out and, if not, at least they will learn to endure their burden together. That is the conventional Stage Three approach to problem solving.

A less common but more sophisticated response to crisis is to begin to question the universality of the belief system. Some partners begin to ask themselves, "If what we believe in doesn't seem to work in this case, then in what other situations might it also fail us?" Such a line of questioning can at times lead the couple across the threshold into Stage Four, where they can emerge into a new and fearful level of maturity, where they can be the judges, and even the creators, of universal principles—rather than merely followers.

4. Friendship marriage dissolves personal identity. By downplaying the unique in favor of the universal, Stage Three relationships tend to set up needless barriers to personal identity and growth. By viewing sex from an essentially pre-adolescent perspective, friendship marriages create a type of spiritual brother-sister bond instead of the more mature and more complex male-female polarity. As a result, partners fail to develop a full awareness of gender differences. They either resort to simplistic role descriptions of the man's place and the woman's place, or else they cover the differences with a veil of universal good will.

Friendship marriage thus acts as a block to the more difficult and more explosive recognition of individual differences, based on both genetic and cultural influences, which first begin to dawn on us in our early adolescent attempts to communicate across the sexual barriers of pre-adolescence.

In the remainder of this chapter we will look more closely at the personal and cultural resources that affect our potential for relationships through our adolescent experiences and the adolescence of the human race.

Risk, Courage, Experiment, Discovery: Path to a New Stage

More and more couples today are realizing that they cannot develop either true intimacy or personal growth by trying to order their relationship by sets of rules or principles supposedly

100

valid in all situations. Couples know that their own relationship is unique. They sense that if their own marriage is to develop its full potential, the two of them must embark on an adventure into a new stage. This stage will require risk, courage, experiment, and discovery to a degree unimagined by those couples nestled comfortably into a friendship marriage.

This new stage of marriage often explodes onto the scene in a couple's life. Sometimes it is sparked when one or both partners undergo a crisis of personal identity. In this crisis one or both partners discover that their earlier shared values no longer suffice.

Sometimes it happens when a husband completes professional training and enters a sophisticated career world. The new world is closed to the wife, even though she has supported him through all the lean years. The couple may have shared the dream of the professional career, but in the outside world the ticket admits only one. The result is a crisis in the relationship. The need for new identity is crying to be met.

Sometimes it's the man who for years contentedly accepts certain roles written for him by parents, wife, children, career, and community. Then as he struggles with a crisis in personal identity, all his relationships are forced to change or die.

Whatever the scenario, the effects of a personal identity search quite often challenge the relationship to its roots. It is the single most common wedge that destroys friendship marriages. Tragically, for people trained to believe that a pre-adolescent friendship model is the highest form of marriage, the only available alternatives are either retreat into an earlier stage or divorce. Those who do not know the difference between the death of a relationship and the birth of a new stage of consciousness miss the opportunity for a new degree of intimacy.

The marriage that is based on a commitment to individual growth represents a new stage in historical and psychological consciousness. It makes the attempt to solve the basic inadequacies of friendship marriage.

Whereas friendship marriages tend to smother conflict, to absorb differences of opinion and personality by appeal to commonly affirmed principles, the partners in a Stage Four marriage recognize that conflicts serve important purposes. They see that conflicts may be opportunities for self-discovery and for breaking through to new levels of intimacy.

New way to look at church conflict

101

Whereas friendship marriages tend to be more spiritual than physical, more practical than passionate, the person-centered marriage tries to have it both ways.

In Stage Four, a relationship fosters the sharing of intimate feelings. Couples seek to experience deep emotions and to communicate with each other about them. They learn to practice a new kind of discipline based on a profoundly new orientation.

Entering Stage Four: Two Requirements

This stage is open to those who have made two primary kinds of discoveries about themselves. One is an interpersonal discovery, in which people begin to comprehend the inequities and complexities of relations between the sexes. The other is a cultural discovery, in which people become aware of the limits and biases of their particular social class. These new inquiries into the sexual and social barriers to intimacy bring people to a crucial period in life. The consequences of this emerging sexual and social consciousness can be either constructive or destructive.

The adolescent period of people's lives often proves decisive in determining both their sexual and their social maturity. Adolescence affects a person's future capacity for deep intimacy more than any of the earlier stages. It is the time when sexual and social awareness develops most rapidly. In pre-adolescence, young people tend to spend most of their time in sexually separate groups. If this practice of sexual separation continues through adolescence, young people are likely to remain in Stage Three relationships through most of their lives. Pre-adolescence also places limits on young people's social awareness. At this age young people get few opportunities to test whether the truths that appear universal to them actually are universal, or whether they are limited and provincial.

For those whose values remain in the conventional Stage Three lifestyle, relationships tend to remain pre-sexual and pre-social. Relationships with the opposite sex tend to be formalized, not in the sense of hard and fast roles, but in conventional understandings of how to deal with masculine and feminine behavior. Within this conventional value system, it is difficult to maintain friendships across sexual lines without either falling into traditional roles or allowing these friendships to take on an erotic connotation. Limitations like these can be overcome, however, if people can emerge from their adolescent experiences with a new sensitivity to sexual and social barriers and to the dynamics that are necessary to overcome them.

The Adolescent Years: Breaking Through Social/Sexual Barriers

No one ever forgets how it feels to be an adolescent. The sense of freedom mingled with the fear of loneliness; the taste of personal power dissolved by plummeting self-esteem; the vented anger neutralized by the need for acceptance. The struggles with personal and social changes were as profound as the biological revolution of puberty. Even though the earlier physical changes were more noticeable, the later changes in the way a person views the world were ultimately more decisive.

Let's begin to define more specifically how adolescents emerge into this new stage where they relate effectively to persons of the opposite sex and of different social classes. In this adolescent stage young people begin to view themselves in a new way. Their own lives become objects of curiosity and study. Young persons between the ages of thirteen and eighteen begin to step outside themselves and try to see their lives from other viewpoints. Adolescents develop a curiosity about what they look like from the viewpoint of the opposite sex. They also begin thinking about how it feels to be someone whose background, culture, and values are different from their own. By stepping outside themselves, they can imagine changes in themselves. They can see potential that is not yet realized.

Young Natural Scientists in the Laboratory of Love

Adolescents also begin to reflect more objectively on their own behavior, feelings, and drives. Like young scientists, they develop skills in the use of hypothesis and experiment. They adopt various stances, poses, or roles, not as the Stage Two person would, in order to be defined and controlled by them, but in order to observe, evaluate, and ultimately choose among the possibilities.

Adolescents also begin to intellectualize about what we generally think of as instinctive behavior. Many heretofore uncontrolled impulses now come into a teenager's awareness. Through study and experimentation, they learn methods of bringing more and more of their natural desires under individual control. Even

103

the experience of falling in love becomes an object of analysis and experiment for adolescents. We do not ordinarily think of teenagers being engaged in the scientific analysis, classification, and interpretation of love. Yet such is the content of most conversations in an adolescent relationship. The young couple goes over and over their own relationship, examining it, classifying it, comparing it to the relationships of others and also to the way it looked to them last week and yesterday. Through these conversations they begin to define, shape, and enrich their relationship.

Young Social Scientists in the Field Study of Intimacy

Learning to observe and control relationships affects adolescents in their expanded awareness of social differences. They come to realize that others have different points of view and that others may change their opinions. Adolescents begin to see that the world is perceived by individuals and cultures through the lens of their own viewpoints, many of who mistakenly believe that their values are universally accepted. Adolescents become intrigued by the necessity to choose among differing, even conflicting, claims to truth. They become fascinated by the many ways the world appears to other people. They realize that people always form opinions about the other persons they meet and that there will never be one way of behavior that will meet the approval of everyone. The only way they can see to find out how to choose values or make decisions is to embark on a venture of trial and error.

To Know Another Person from the Inside Out

Adolescents try to experience another person not just from their own point of view but from that other person's unique point of view. They try to get into another person's skin, to understand a person from the inside out, not just from the outside in. In adolescence a person begins to develop the potential to separate the external self that others see from the inner self that only one person sees. It becomes possible temporarily to suppress one's sense of the "other" in a person. It becomes possible to open oneself to the other person's point of view, to set aside one's own notion of what the world looks like.

The Purpose of Unconventional Lifestyles

There is a reason why adolescents begin to develop a lifestyle that is qualitatively different from the conventional behavior of their earlier life. Adolescents are beginning to realize the need to develop a personal outlook or faith, one that can support them in their loneliest or most alienated moments. They also know that if their outlook proves to be different from those that prevail in conventional society, they must be ready for their personal perspective to be challenged by others. They may be challenged by others. They may even be challenged by other adolescents.

So a certain vulnerability and defensiveness sets in when an adolescent seeks to develop independent judgment. Young persons often feel the need to justify the truth and adequacy of their views. They may hold themselves and their friends accountable for developing relationships that meet the new test of truth. In Stage Four, the test of truth is not whether it makes universal claims but whether it offers inner consistency and authenticity. Under this test adolescents often seek a thought-out set of reasons for behaving the way they do. They look for a philosophy that holds things together, one that helps them feel free either to stand alone or to stand with others.

Being Unconventional Together

While adolescents seek to be independent, often they will join others who they believe are making the same journey. Adolescents band together for different purposes, however, than do pre-adolescents. Adolescents get together, sometimes by the tens of thousands, to search for individuality. Becoming their own persons does not necessarily separate adolescents from their earlier peer groups or family relationships. Instead, they shift toward a more autonomous outlook toward these group activities. They feel more confident about picking and choosing what they will accept and affirm and what they will repudiate or modify among the values and associations that have been handed down to them.

The Plight of the 40-Year-Old Teenager

The transition to Stage Four usually begins in the early or middle teens, and it lasts at least through the late teens to early twenties. It is such a difficult and complex transition that it may

105

be protracted throughout the rest of a person's life. Millions of persons today were never able to develop these capacities during their teens; they may not make these discoveries until their thirties or forties. The longer people wait before experiencing these breakthroughs, the fewer people of their own age they will have around them to give their support. Therefore, a profound disruptiveness usually accompanies the change. Sometimes a conventional adult of age thirty to forty suddenly breaks out of the Stage Three conventional lifestyle and adopts a highly individualistic one. When it happens, the break is usually more extreme and more difficult than it would be when a group of teenagers are making the same kind of explorations together. A feeling of break-up accompanies the feeling of breakthrough when an adult makes a belated entry into Stage Four consciousness.

Dikaiosune: Liberty and Justice in Marriage

The developments in the concept of love that emerge within Stage Four are drawn from both the adolescent stage of history and the adolescent stage of the individual. The Stage Four concept of love is a relationship built upon justice, fairness, and equality as prerequisites for intimacy. The Greek or biblical word for this is *dikaiosune*. It is sometimes translated as righteousness, sometimes as justice. *Dikaiosune* refers to right relationships, both between God and man and within human life. It denotes behavior that is characteristic of righteous ideals or qualities. The biblical prophets appealed to the divine qualities of justice— *dikaiosune*—in calling for the reform of the corrupt and callous society that Israel had become. Paul the apostle based his teaching about justification by faith on the *dikaiosune*, or righteousness, of God, which is absolute and not affected by human unrighteousness. The Protestant concepts of individual salvation and social justice stem from the recovery of the concept of *dikaiosune* by Martin Luther, John Calvin, and other reformers. Through the Protestant tradition, as we have seen, the new Stage Four ideal for love relationships has permeated our culture.

A Stage Four marriage recognizes that balance is the center of love. Love cannot flourish when one partner expects to receive more than he or she gives. Intimacy cannot grow when one person tries to use power to coerce love from another. Love must

106

be based on justice, on equality, on *dikaiosune*. Stage Four emphasizes the fact that love is a voluntary act, offered freely between equals. Love is recognized as a force so powerful that it can break down the barriers set up between the sexes by the traditional roles and conventions of our culture.

Love expressed as justice demands far more from a couple than does the Stage One need for survival or the Stage Two acceptance of roles and rules or the Stage Three appeal to universal principles. Love imbued with justice seeks a relationship devoted to a mutual adventure in self-discovery. This is not to say that Stage Four couples demand total equality in every area for each partner. Rather, they share a deep sensitivity to balanced and fair treatment. Their relationship is primarily centered in a delicate balance of giving and receiving. Love is expressed not in terms of a rigid reordering of gender roles but rather in an adventure in which both partners seek to develop their potential to the fullest. The two people express their love for each other by encouraging each other to grow.

That usually means overthrowing many of the concepts generally considered universally true about masculinity and feminity. Sometimes they will act in conventional ways, but that is because they choose to do so and not because they are yielding to social pressure. And sometimes they will choose highly unconventional ways, not out of a desire to be different or to shock other people but because these unconventional approaches meet their deepest personal needs. Whether their behavior is viewed as conventional or unconventional, the Stage Four couple is seeking to develop a person-centered relationship.

The Person-Centered Marriage
Partners in a person-centered marriage learn to be objective about their subjective feelings. They learn to employ the inductive methods of science in dealing with each other's needs. They no longer base their assumptions about each other on some kind of *a priori* knowledge of human nature. Rather, they seek descriptive knowledge of each other which comes from personal observation and experience.

Stage Four requires a couple to place a premium on good communication skills. Verbal clarity and listening skills are the

[margin notes, handwritten]: ministry of equals very tricky to the 2 me / last words of the church "that's what we pay the pastor for!"

precision instruments of the new scientific consciousness. Partners need to develop the ability to express their feelings clearly and often. They also need to develop new listening skills. Since the couple is no longer content with exchanging platitudes and commonly held beliefs, they will seek ways to express the uniquely personal feelings that they have never experienced or expressed before.

The Stage Four marriage offers two people the opportunity to discover how an intimate relationship can actually enhance their potential for self-knowledge and can do so far better than a solitary quest. Two people together work better than one alone in developing the skills needed for disciplined inquiry into one's own motivations, goals, and needs. Each can help the other look through the smoke screens and the avoidance techniques that the psyche throws up to ward off trespassers. The more two people learn to trust each other, the richer the shared experience and the shared vocabulary become.

Couples who move into Stage Four learn to tell when a new stage is about to begin in their relationship. They are not as likely to fear newness, nor are they as likely to mistake change for impending breakup. When a Stage Four couple begin to sense some dead ends or limitations in their relationship, they aren't as likely to panic and to deny their feelings. By now, having been through at least three crises that appeared at first to be the signs of divorce, they are more ready to wait calmly for some aspects of their relationship to die, while new, more deeply satisfying dimensions are about to be born.

Coping with Unpleasant Truths

When couples develop new powers of observation, verbalization, and listening, their ability to be objective about their feelings may bring them face to face with previously hidden prejudices, defenses, and self-defeating habits. They begin to discover the extent of their biases. Discovering these unpleasant truths long buried can become the rewards of Stage Four marriage, truths which a Stage Three couple would just as soon keep buried.

One of these truths is the realization that a kind of uncertainty principle often operates in a relationship. It is like the principle of physics that states that an observer interferes with the behavior of the observed subject by the very act of observation. The physicists are referring to the behavior of subatomic particles, but couples can use it to shed light on interpersonal relations. Stage Four couples come to realize that males and females cannot always completely enter one another's worlds. The very presence of a member of the opposite sex can interfere with a person's behavior. Sometimes this discovery discourages a person from continuing the adventure. But for those couples who persevere, a new level of understanding is waiting.

Another discovery that challenges Stage Four couples is the tendency toward "creeping ideologies." After giving up the Stage Three reliance on universal principles as a framework for understanding life, partners often are tempted to devise a new framework of "individual universals"—truths that work for me, even if they don't work for you. So a new ideology creeps in: It could be astrology, a new religion, a hobby or a career. Its effect is to separate the partners, to leave one partner outside the new framework. If the other partner is to keep abreast, he or she must learn the new vocabulary and accept the new ground rules, or else lose out. In the name of "individual personality development," one person shuts out the other, and trades an affair with an ideology for intimacy with another person.

The Delights of Continuous Growth
Nothing is ultimately as boring as living with a person who thinks he or she has gotten it all together. Fortunately, that is never a reality for two persons who build a relationship based on continuous individual growth. The temptation is always there, however, to retreat into a safer, earlier stage. The mature alternative is to grow with each other into a new stage. Growth together will be the inevitable consequence for lovers who deepen their sense of trust, open communication, and mutual affirmation. When a couple reaches the point where both partners can present their own self-deceptions to each other without fear of being attacked, they have taken the first step across a boundary where a still newer stage of consciousness awaits them.

What About the Impact of Liberation Ideology?
The Stage Four marriage is unavoidably bound up with liberation ideology. That may as well be said forthrightly. It is based on the cultural ideal of rejecting a vision of a golden past, and

constructing a model never before realized. The model of a marriage built upon justice, however, has few cultural supports from conventional society. It is tragically the case that when a man or woman first confronts liberation ideology and tries to live by the ideals it has spawned, neither the woman nor the man can readily cope with it, especially if each comes out of a Stage Three conventional background. Liberation ideology has often been blamed for the breakup of conventional marriages. A person who views the breakup of a conventional Stage Three marriage can express only bewilderment as to what could have caused it. From the conventional viewpoint, a marriage may seem to have been ideal, when in reality both partners were being strangled by the suffocatingly complacent attitudes around them. From the viewpoint of Stage Two, marriages usually break up over someone's refusal to play to traditional roles. A Stage Two personality brands liberation as an enemy, a threat, and classifies it as a destroyer of the household. Those who have tasted the joys of personal freedom and mutual encouragement to grow know better. But it is often impossible to explain it to those who are locked into earlier stages.

How then is it possible for two people to come into contact with liberation ideology and to stay together? One key is the degree to which both partners have learned to be sensitive to justice and injustice among groups and individuals in the society as a whole. Another factor is the extent of their experience, especially in their adolescent dating period, with the differences in the needs of men and women. Instead of the opposites in the opposite sex coming as explosive new truths, they are seen as realities that have been discovered years earlier during the person's adolescence. If the two persons have been exposed to a sensitivity for fairness, for *dikaiosune*, then they are more likely to make this transition. They are better prepared to build their own model for a relationship. They can choose to be either conventional or unconventional. They can choose to play out certain roles and break away from other roles, taking some and leaving others as they please.

The difference lies in the couple's freedom to make independent choices from among the alternatives spread before them, rather than having to accept circumstances imposed upon them from forces of culture and childhood experience. Because this is

110

the case, the couple whose relationship is based on fairness and on independence develop confidence that they can achieve in their relationship what they can envision in their minds. So it is possible for people who develop a Stage Four relationship to build a far stronger, more durable, more intimate marriage than would be possible under the limitations of the earlier stages.

The Future of Liberated Marriage

Rather than accept the alarms being set off by those who are threatened by marriage based on *dikaiosune*, I will venture to predict that we may, in fact, begin to see a diminishing of the divorce rate in America in the next few years. So far we have seen what happens when the ideals of the Stage Four liberation consciousness first collide with Stage Three conventional consciousness.

When couples in conventional marriages first began to face the need for change, the culture around them failed to offer support for advancing to Stage Four. This first wave of acquaintance with the concept of love as *dikaiosune* was viewed as dangerous and threatening, explosive and disintegrating. But the final word is not yet in concerning liberation ideology and its effect on love relationships. Many signs indicate that our culture as a whole is moving from Stage Three to Stage Four. As it does so, we may begin to see that a new generation of individuals who were reared in a Stage Four emphasis on independence and personal growth will begin to appreciate the potential that is there for a new depth in love relationships. This potential may well prove strong enough to bring people together for lifelong growth within marriage. We may not be forced to continue watching helplessly as marriage and family buckle and sag under this era of disturbance, change, and anxiety.

In spite of the lack of cultural supports for personal-growth marriage, a large number of people have been able to make the leap. Even larger numbers of people may be expected to do so in the future. There is thus a basis for confidence that the present statistics about divorce in America are not a sign of a coming total disintegration. A more optimistic future may be discerned as experts examine the nature of second marriages. Second marriages are not as stable as first marriages, but the reasons for their dissolution are different. Many conventional first marriages are

111

breaking up over the discovery of individual freedom and the search for ideology. They are breaking up over the failure to integrate adolescent values into the relationship. These are the goals that motivate many in their second marriages. The hope is that what the older generation has chosen as an ideal for second marriages, the younger generation may achieve the first time around. Independence and personal growth will not appear as lonely, individual searches inimical to lasting relationships. Decisions about marriage will emerge out of a cultural background where equality, liberation, and the development of a coherent personal philosophy are undertaken by lovers rather than loners.

Becoming More Sensitive to Stage Four Marriage: Lovers Do It Better than Loners

Marriage based on the ideals presented in this chapter can offer the best possible environment for personal growth. If "lovers are better than loners" in encouraging individual freedom, it is because lovers provide each other with opportunities for feedback, for measurement, for affirmation. Liberation can emerge without tearing at the fabric of relationships. Communication of one's deepest longings and worst fears, shared with someone who is unconditionally accepting of both strengths and weaknesses, is the starting point for declaring independence at the most intimate levels of one's being. For couples who want to venture further into a marriage that encourages personal growth and independence, here are some points of contact to draw you closer to the goal:

1. Tell each other about your experiences within the limitations of your social environment. Have you had, and do you have, good friends whose economic status is considerably higher or lower than yours? What about friends of another race, religious outlook, educational level, age difference? Share with each other the enjoyments and the problems you find in friendships across social barriers.

2. Talk about the differences in your attitudes toward sexuality. Share how you differ in your views of the roles of the sexes. Discuss your differences regarding your sexual needs. Tell each other how you feel about having close friends of the opposite sex.

Is it possible to do so without causing strains in your marriage? What about close friends of the same sex? Is it easier to confide in them than in your spouse, or is it more difficult?

3. Try to recall and share the last time your spouse said something to you that was truly new, unexpected, or unpredictable. Is it possible that you get into ruts with each other? When you listen to each other, do you listen only for what is readily understandable? Or do you look for new, unexpected content and tone? Tell each other ways in which your listening habits can help and hinder adventures into new, untried areas of communication.

4. Nearly everybody grows up believing something is accepted as universally true, only to find that many respected persons do not agree. Share with each other some important value you once believed to be absolutely true, but later came to modify. What factors most affected your change? In what area of your life is a significant change now taking place in your attitude about important values from the past?

5. Tell your spouse some ways he or she has encouraged you toward personal growth. Do you feel this encouragement was for your own good, or because your spouse wanted you to change?

6. Here's a way to test the differences between objective and subjective perceptions. Each of you in turn suggest what seems to you to be inconsistent behavior in your spouse. Does your spouse agree with your perception? How is it possible to compare your own view of your behavior with the view of another person? Do the two of you try to resolve the differences between subjective and objective perceptions? Do you ever try to encourage differing perceptions of deeply personal behavior? When was the last time?

7. Think of something you've accomplished that no one in your family has ever done before. Share your feelings about this achievement with your spouse.

8. In every relationship, some areas of life are seemingly in balance, while others seem unfairly stacked in favor of one partner or the other. Try to exchange with each other one aspect of your life which seems unfairly advantageous to your spouse. Share any feelings of resentment you have (if they are ready to surface at this time). Then tell each other how it feels to be able to express the resentment instead of holding it in.

9. All growth experiences seemingly require risk, courage, and pain. What is the most important area of personal growth each of you has experienced in the last twelve months? Reflect with each other on at least one specific element that involved (a) risk, (b) courage, and (c) pain. Try to think of at least one way this particular experience has strained your relationship and at least one way your marriage has been strengthened by it.

Selected Reading for Background and Discussion

Stage Four

The Rise of Political Independence and Individualism

Gordon Allport, *The Individual and His Religion*
Carl Rogers, *Becoming Partners*
Rollo May, *Love and Will*
Richard N. Bolles, *What Color Is Your Parachute?*
Reay Tannehill, *Sex in History*
William James, *The Varieties of Religious Experience*
Letha Scanzoni and Nancy Hardesty, *All We're Meant to Be: A Biblical Approach to Women's Liberation*
Rene Dubos, *Beast or Angel*
Marshall McLuhan, *The Gutenberg Galaxy*
Wayne Oates, *Psychology of Religion*
Hans Kung, *On Being a Christian*
Max Weber, *The Sociology of Religion*

Stage Five: *Agape,* Love Greater than the Sum of Its Parts

The Post-Adolescent Period of a Relationship

LGBTQIA
Immigrants
or Kenmend
Kenosis!

To be vulnerable is to suffer loss,
to have to learn how to grieve.
It is to lose immunity
against the cries, laughs, and songs of others.
When we become vulnerable,
we are accessible to be known.
        —Robert Raines, *Living the Questions*[9]

The paradox of *agape,* of self-giving love,
        is that it does the impossible,
        the thing we have just said
        cannot be done.
It shares the unshareable,
        gives the ungiveable,
        and receives from the other
        the gift that can no more
        be received than given:
        the gift of self,
        the gift of the giver,
        the I.

115

Agape, as distinct from *eros* (desire)
or *philia* (friendship) or *storge* (affection),
is not a gift just of pleasure,
    or the body,
    or possessions,
    or time, or actions,
    or interests, or feelings, or thoughts,
    but of self.
—Peter Kreeft, *Love Is Stronger than Death*[10]

The goal and the dream that is set before millions of couples today is to be absorbed in a relationship that encourages and enhances personal growth. That dream seems more than enough to challenge and compel us, especially in a time when so many people feel they are being forced to choose between the health of their relationship and their development as persons.

Increasingly, however, couples are discovering that personal growth in marriage is not enough. Some of those who manage to create a relationship that gives more individual identity than it takes away still find themselves filled with a deep sense of unease and even anxiety. Viewed from the outside, these couples would appear to have made the dream of so many come true for themselves. So to hear couples express their deep apprehensions about the limits and drawbacks of a relationship based on personal growth causes surprise, disappointment, or even anger among others who are still striving to realize the dream.

The apprehensions are based on warning signals. Some of these warning signals come from out of the past. Inner voices left over from Stage Three may continue to suggest that personal growth relationships are selfish, are destructive of conventional values, undermine traditional family life, and cut people off from their less adventurous friends and family members.

But there are other signals that seem to increase in their insistency the longer a couple enjoys the intimacy that is possible in a post-conventional relationship. These signals are coming from the future. They are beckoning couples to take yet another adventure together, one that is more perilous but even more rewarding than anything they've yet experienced. The cost: another "divorce," the death of their gratifying individualistic habits, and yet another prolonged period of painful, frightening disequilibrium.

116

As with all the previous stage changes, this one begins not with a siren song to an appealing new alternative but with disquieting signs that there are limits to what the present stage can offer. If there is no turning back to earlier levels of comfort, then there is only one choice: Either resist the signals or decide to heed them.

The "Fourth Divorce": Beyond Personal Growth
The first wave of Stage Five signals reaches a couple precisely because they have developed such a finely tuned sensitivity to fairness and justice, to the imperatives of the liberated consciousness. The message these signals send, however, is that liberation has its limits—limits that have nothing to do with the often repeated complaints and attacks from preliberation mentalities. Because a couple has struggled so heroically to break free of the limitations of conventional marriage, they may not be in a position at first to distinguish which signals come from the future and which from the past. Inevitably, however, the new messages do get through and make a firm, if threatening, place for themselves. These messages strike at the very heart of a couple's hard-earned liberation and self-discovery by raising questions about the means they have used. Growing doubts are raised about the kind of knowledge of each other that comes from the personal search.

Getting Beyond Trial and Error
The fact is that Stage Four knowledge is experimental knowledge, based on trial and error, observation, empirical testing. As a result, what lovers have learned about themselves and each other tends to focus on information, collected data, predictable patterns. At a certain point, qualms begin to arise about the idea of using persons in experiments—not only in terms of the limits on the levels of knowledge attained thereby, but also in terms of the moral and spiritual quality of the intimacy they have achieved. Rarely is a couple's dawning awareness expressed in such intellectual terms, of course; more frequently it comes at the end of a long, slow emotional malaise, erupting into a compulsion to try a series of consciousness-raising experiments. In the end comes a realization that simply compiling more information, merely acquiring more experiences, will fail to lead into a new level of intimacy. To the contrary, it leads to dissatisfaction with oneself,

117

one's partner, even with the adventure of intimacy itself. Then often comes a withdrawal, a disengagement, an alienation, first from other persons, then from unattractive aspects of oneself, until one is finally left in a kind of moral autism. Clearly, no relationship can long withstand such a shriveling of loving experiences.

Relating Without Manipulating

The quest for personal knowledge too often results in merely analytical truth, the kind that comes from taking things apart. What is missing is a means of attaining a synthesis, putting together a pattern of meaning out of the many partial, experiential, experimental truths. By viewing others and oneself as objects, we arrive at objective truth, only to discover that objective truth is a dialectical opposite of the kind of truth to be enjoyed and enlarged through personal relationships.

Clearly, urgently, the search must go on for a non-manipulative means of relating to persons, a way that discovers and enhances personal worth, dignity and potentiality. There must be a way to love that helps us stop treating the other partner as a puzzle to be solved, and shows us how to treat one another as infinite yet uniquely personal mysteries to be contemplated. When two people arrive at such a point in their personal quests and in their relationship, the signals from the new stage become louder and more insistent. And when this happens, the next period of disequilibrium, the next divorce within the marriage, has begun.

This time, however, the impact will be different. That is because the couple already has weathered a series of crises, and has seen that each period of unsettling is followed by a richer and more deeply satisfying stage in the relationship. By now it is possible actually to welcome the oncoming fourth "divorce," to let it work its way toward the new plateau.

The Three Couples: Beyond Liberation

To illustrate some ways this new divorce can offset a marriage, we can view it through the eyes of our three couples.

Allen and Barbara

Their life together up to this point has seemed to be a series of minor crises, as one challenge after another forced Allen and

Barbara to find the courage to face inevitable change. They have overcome crises of identity and crises of vocation. Through countless daily tests of their commitment to each other, they have emerged into a relationship that offers even more deeply satisfying pleasures.

The ultimate test, however, was yet to come. Allen was diagnosed as having cancer of the lymph glands, an especially fast-spreading type with only a 50 percent remission rate.

The life-threatening aspects of the catastrophe were not, it turned out, the most terrifying ones. When a person dies, society develops a ritual-like procedure to deal with the shock. But a long critical illness that does not end in quick death proceeds into the realm of the unpredictable where no rules apply, where people's responses are unregulated by custom.

Through their early days of absorbing the blows, the creative, lovingly intimate world Allen and Barbara had built together seemed a cruel mockery instead of a sustaining power. Nothing they had accomplished up to now could survive the death or even the long-term disability of either partner. Love, it began to appear, was even more fragile than life itself, a rose garden to tend, not a rock foundation to build upon. These two intelligent, sensitive adults each found themselves awakened in the night by their own crying out, their own feelings of rage, futility, and despair. Which was worse, they wondered, to be the one who dies and leaves all this behind, or to be the one left behind in the rubble. Slowly, painfully, they began to adjust to the merciless new realities.

For Allen it was an endless series of excruciating therapies, his body a ravaged field where the rebellious hordes were destroyed by invading armies in countless battles. For Barbara, the new reality spelled the end of her life as a crusader and parent. She rejoined the job force, this time selling real estate, the most lucrative way she knew of for taking on the role of sole provider. Their daughter spent most after-school time with Allen's parents.

As the radiation and chemotherapies bought a little time, the days of suspension between life and death dragged into weeks and then months. Still, no routines and patterns could be established. Life revolved around a giant question mark.

After nearly two years, doctors could begin to predict that the cancer was in tactical retreat. Nobody with cancer is ever "healed" as they are if it were a broken arm; "in remission" is the chilling, daring-to-hope term most often employed. But the new extension did provide a measure of respite. Allen found himself offering to teach drawing to the children in the hospital's cancer ward, an experience that enabled him to see that even in the face of death, beauty is a human impulse that should be encouraged, not stifled. As for Barbara, even in her real estate selling, she began to find ways to allow her humanitarian impulses a place to play, helping families make lifestyle decisions. As the two of them could spend more time at home, and their daughter could rejoin the family, they came to realize what elements in their life together could survive a brush with death, and what could not.

Even now Allen and Barbara live each day under a death threat. What they've built still might suddenly collapse. The difference is, now they know that after all the energy, all the sacrifice, and all the risk, their love is stronger than rage, stronger than despair, stronger than death.

Charlie and Donna

The two greatest personal triumphs Charlie and Donna had ever experienced both occurred in the same week. And neither of them ever recovered from the blows. First, Donna's father announced to her that he was willing to help her start a new restaurant chain, one that would bear her name and personal stamp. He was able to assemble a group of investors who would back her with a first-year commitment of three million dollars. Then, only three days later, Charles was chosen, over several more experienced agents, to head a new district being developed in the fast-growing affluent suburbs of Los Angeles, along the beautiful Pacific Coast.

In shock from the two revelations, Charlie and Donna couldn't absorb the full impact for a couple of days. Donna's great breakthrough tied her in securely with the local Friendsdale financial community. Charlie's once-in-a-lifetime opportunity opened to him the personal contacts—and personal fortunes—of Palm Springs society, the Silicone Valley computer and defense establishment, and the booming Irvine real estate developers (not to mention living in the "Playground of the West." Surely they'd find a way for both of their dreams to come true.

First they tried a commuter marriage, the kind they'd read about between "bi-coastal" celebrities with dual careers in Hollywood and on Broadway. With their lives changing so rapidly, however, there wasn't enough time on the weekends to catch up with it all. And the demands for long hours at work showed no signs of letting up. The cross-country commutes, so exciting at first, began to take their toll, slowing to alternate weekends, and finally monthly visits, before they ceased altogether.

Within the year Charlie and Donna were separated. Charlie shifted permanently to California, and Donna moved in with her parents in their spacious new lakefront home. It was no peaceful separation, and it was no final solution to a painful situation of long standing. The paradox of career success above their wildest dreams, combined with a relationship failure beyond their worst fears, proved an explosive mixture. The affect on Charlie was violent. Late-night phone calls, screaming and sobbing, threatening and pleading, kept him functioning well below his capabilities, draining his drive and raising real doubts in his mind that he could cope with either success or failure. Donna's reaction was to withdraw deep within herself, where she could nurse her wounds in solitude. With her father she thrived on the new relationship as business partner.

Eventually Charlie bought a condominium for himself and a pretty blond office worker. A new life began without his having to dwell on or in the past. Together Charlie and his secretary could start something that didn't need answers to too many questions in order to flourish. Here at least was a relationship built on something besides competition.

For Donna's part, the divorce freed her to become the successful restaurateur. It wasn't necessary to start an entangling alliance with a man in order to get ahead. She could make it on her own, alone but not lonely, in a man's world.

Eddie and Fran

Some of their longtime friends had a lot of good-natured fun at their expense when Eddie and Fran announced their intention to get married. After the wedding, however, the friends gradually began to drift away, as Eddie settled into a low-paying steady job driving a delivery van, and Fran closed out her day care work to await the birth of their first child.

Not long after their son was born, Eddie and Fran moved into a better neighborhood where other young couples were spending their time working hard rearing children, fixing TV

121

dinners, going to bed early, and caring for lawns on the weekends. It was like life on a different planet compared to the way they'd always lived, the way they'd been brought up. If their former friends could see them now, they'd be a little ashamed, a little saddened, to see these two free spirits pouring such energy into the straight life. The paradox would be lost on these friends: that the friends were the ones living out predictable roles, that Eddie and Fran were the ones who'd created a new life, made a free choice, taken a real risk. Eddie and Fran themselves only dimly recognized the irony. If pressed or teased or needled, Eddie's response would be to nod and smile, and without emotion to reply with vulgar epithet. With that, for him, the paradox was resolved.

Three Couples Coming to Terms with Paradox

Into the life of every marriage inevitably comes a crisis of paradox. It is a crisis where two seemingly contradictory, irreconcilable forces come in from opposite directions and challenge all the couple's most hard-earned assumptions and values, leaving them at the mercy of whatever dangers lie buried at the core of their relationship, away from their control. It is this crisis of paradox that has just attacked the three marriages related on the pages above.

The simplest way to approach paradox is to develop a sense of irony, a sense of black humor. The ironies of the plights of the three couples are manifest:

—Allen and Barbara have been stripped of their creativity, and apparently reduced to a struggle for survival and to a return to hated constricting roles.

—Charlie and Donna both are winning their competitive struggles, yet are unable to share the thrill of victory.

—Eddie and Fran are moving up from the counter-culture, up toward middle-class respectability, reversing the conventional process.

All the couples are vulnerable to an ironist's twist. Yet all are deserving of a worthier response than an ironist can offer. The cynic and the ironist will fail to look deeply enough into these situations to view the truth at its most paradoxical. What they see is only apparent reality. Out of sight of the ironist's glance lie deeper truths.

122

Allen and Barbara only appear to be struggling for survival and role-playing. They have discovered a rare bond of intimacy, a spiral staircase that opens all the stages and levels of their relationship to them at once.

In losing each other, Charlie and Donna have preserved the only relationship that either of them could sustain at this time of their lives: an inner truce between warring forces that must be tamed and trained before they can be yoked together for life with another person.

And Eddie and Fran? It would be presumptuous to criticize their quiet heroism, the courageous use of their meager inherited resources, their efforts to create order where chaos had ruled.

Only by going beyond cynicism, by developing a tool more useful than the ironic twist, can a person look into the new paradoxical reality that beckons us toward this the deeper level of living that becomes possible inside Stage Five.

Marks of Post-Adolescent Consciousness

Contradictory claims are all around us, of course, and most of us have long since developed ways to deal with them. We may filter out what doesn't fit our needs or predispositions and accept what squares with our own perceptions. We may hear the competing claims, but not at the level of intensity or depth or seriousness that the proclaimers would like.

In Stage Five, however, we are given new resources. We can hear the strident, conflicting claims. We learn to accept what we hear the way that it is sent, without censoring or rearranging it to fit our own prejudices. We comprehend the claims, no matter how self-defeating or self-contradictory they seem, at a level of intensity, depth, and seriousness that approaches, or even exceeds, the level at which the proclaimers are operating.

Such a degree of empathy is impossible before Stage Five, because until this point we have lacked these crucial resources that only now became available:

1. The capacity for accepting paradox (truths that appear contradictory, such as the words of Jesus that the least shall be the greatest or the servant shall be the leader);

2. The ability to live comfortably in a pluralistic world, a world where many claims are made to ultimate truth, without yielding to any of the claims and without giving up the search;

123

3. The habit of thinking dialectically (challenging every claim by determining what its opposite claim might be, and examining whether the opposite might also be true).

How do these three resources make a difference? The different ways we understand the statement "the least shall be the greatest" will serve to illustrate.

The Stage One personality fails to see anything contradictory in the saying. The fact that it is a word from the Lord is enough to establish its authority, whatever its meaning.

In Stage Two, the statement is viewed dualistically (There are two kinds of people in the world, the least and the greatest, and we must get on the right side).

In Stage Three, we discover a higher principle to live by, that service is the route to spiritual greatness—a principle that makes logical sense out of the apparent contradiction.

Stage Four offers a new, more socially conscious perspective, in which we come to realize that the world does not operate by this higher principle. The "least" are still on the bottom. Therefore, the power structures must be transformed so that the true servants of the people will rule, and the selfish powerful are brought down.

Stage Five, with its capacity to see several "truths" at once, accepts all the elements of truth in each of the previous stages, and also sees even more. Stage Five helps us discover, for instance, that all the earlier stages tend to deny the truths of each previous stage. Growth into each new stage seems to require the rejection of what came earlier. Inherent in these denials is a significant loss, a loss of whatever germ of truth lay in the insights of each earlier stage. As a result, each time we moved into a new stage, we became trapped in a form of moral elitism, a feeling of superiority toward all that has gone before. This denial of what is different also tended to blind us to truth that is yet to be discovered. It brought us an element of suspicion toward whatever is new. The pain of growth, and the difficulties of escaping old, destructive habits, made us wary that any new way might turn out to be nothing more than some old, rejected view in disguise.

In contrast, Stage Five helps us internalize each of the previous stages. We learn how to accept responsibility for the lingering effects of the earlier stages that are still within us. We no longer see "Stage One people" *out there*, but see the same tendencies in ourselves, tendencies we can never overcome.

Thus we begin a new adventure of reclaiming the lost parts of ourselves.

The chaos of Stage One need not be controlled by the roles and rules of Stage Two. Now we can accept our inner chaos as a positive benefit. We can see it as the subconscious pool of our creative energy.

The passion for order and discipline common to Stage Two no longer needs to be softened by the conventions of Stage Three. We can learn to "control our need for control"—to blend it with our creative forces as a necessary step to fresh thinking.

The search for universal principles that was at the heart of Stage Three no longer needs to be tamed by the personal growth needs of Stage Four. We can get back in touch with the universal questions as a way of eliminating the small, trivial issues that wear us down.

We can make a similar reclamation of Stage Four, using its emphasis on personal style to help us find our own unique, creative, disciplined responses to the ultimate questions.

After we've removed the barriers between the stages, and let them all loose to come rushing back into our consciousness again, we experience a new level of wholeness that is the distinctive gift of Stage Five. We affirm all the earlier stages, conflicts and all. We see that the parts add up to something greater than ever—a wholeness of life that is truly "greater than the sum of its parts." The new sense of empathy begins to absorb all of the earlier stages, so that we lose the sense of "we" and "they" inherent in all the earlier stages. At the point of my recognition of this discovery, I am rendered useless for either side of the war, useless *except* for being able to understand, and communicate with, and possibly heal, the combatants.

Even though the physiological resources for developing post-adolescent consciousness are given to us in our late teens and early twenties, it takes the rest of our lives even to begin to tap the full potential we've been given. That is because the principal gift of Stage Five is not primarily intellectual, emotional, or behavioral. Rather, what we receive is a deeper capacity for empathy, for understanding beyond our experience.

Empathy is the result of having experienced a larger measure of suffering and injustice. No amount of information or reflection will suffice. Empathy is the prize we receive for bearing the burdens of responsibility, commitment, failure, and grief in behalf of a love relationship. Empathy is the result of having been thrown into situations for which we were grossly unprepared, and yet, in desperation, finding the resources previously hidden from us that helped us to cope, and even flourish. It is this discovery of hidden resources—of truths that we once neglected as being immature, contradictory, or unconventional—that marks the passage into a life of love as defined in Stage Five.

In our early personality development all of us were either hurried past or held back from experiences that would have made our maturation a smoother process. Then as adults, especially in our relationships, we find ourselves running into a wall. We soon discover that the relationship cannot progress because of the unfinished business of our earlier personality stages. Our relationships cannot mature until our personalities mature.

We might prefer to get on with the work of making a name for ourselves, doing the "adult" business of marriage, family, career, and avoiding reminders of our childish or adolescent ways of dealing with problems. But our relationships keep us honest.

They teach us that no matter how hard we try, we cannot grow a relationship that is more mature than we are.

The Meaning of *Agape*

The expression of love that is appropriate to this stage is represented by the Greek word *agape*. We may translate it into English as "caring" or "compassion" or "unconditional love." In the primitive stage, we remember, love was perceived as sacrifice or loss. It was seen as something painful and therefore not to be sought or expanded. In the second or legal stage, love was seen as a tradeoff, as an agreement. We might have tended to be rather cautious about giving love, because we felt that giving without receiving would result in emotional impoverishment or rejection. In the third stage, we saw that love was based on the discovery of universal values. Brotherly love reaches out and touches our common experiences and resonates with them, yet lacks the resources to transcend the universal values and celebrate the particular, the unique. We found in the fourth stage that love could

126

be the highest expression of personal power, while suffering from all the limitations of experimental, objective knowledge. Now, in the fifth stage, it becomes possible for still newer dimensions of caring to unfold between us, in a new relationship where the spontaneous converges with the profound.

Love that is transformed by *agape* enables a man and woman to give themselves totally to each other, in a way that yields to each of us, and to the relationship, even more than we have given. This is the love that is greater than the sum of its parts.

Agape love transcends the Stage Four attempt to discover potential or potency. A "potent" individual as defined by *agape* is one who cannot keep from giving. If a person cannot give, then he or she is impotent in a relational sense (and sometimes in a physical sense as well). A woman acting in consciousness of *agape* love cannot help giving, spontaneously, intimately, and from her depths. Such love is spiritually analogous to the experience of childbirth. The mother cannot resist giving nurture to the unborn child within her. She spontaneously gives milk to the newborn infant. To refuse these lifegiving impulses would be painful to her or even dangerous. These biological necessities, by the time Stage Five emerges, have become spiritual and psychological imperatives. Whoever is capable of giving freely without fearing loss is on the way to experiencing *agape*. Those who are unable to give are the most deprived of all.

Caring love is able to break through the barriers of economic and social class, yet not be consumed by these issues. The classic examples of *agape* that have been preserved in our religion, art, and literature treat Stage Four social concerns with an apparently casual disregard. From the biblical stories of the Widow's Mite and the Good Samaritan to the Albert Schweitzers and the Mother Theresas of our time, the art of giving has transcended the usual definitions of justice and oppression, wealth and poverty. According to these cultural symbols of *agape*, any situation in which one is deprived of the joy of giving, including a wealthy person's greed or a poor person's insecurity, blocks the possibilities for *agape* love to spread.

Agape tends to destroy hierarchical relationships by ignoring them. In Stage Four hierarchies fell by means of revolutions for social justice. *Agape*, however, destroys chains of command by

127

rendering them useless, by transcending them, by pulling the many levels of a hierarchy toward a new center.

When we give of ourselves, we give what is most precious to us. We give what is most alive in us. We give away our joy, our interests, our understanding, our knowledge, our humor, our sadness, and our fears. In giving as much as we can of ourselves, we enrich both ourselves and others. We enhance our own sense of aliveness.

Giving in the sense of *agape* is pure joy. It's not necessary to assure ourselves that the giving will be reciprocal. In the very act of giving we receive. In giving we cannot help but bring to life something new in the other person. What is brought to life in that other person reflects back upon the giver. And thus we make the other person also a giver. Both the giver and the receiver can share in celebrating what we together have brought to life.

Giving loses its patronizing effects in *agape*, for both persons are givers and both are receivers. Yet it is more than a legal or interpersonal transaction. The act of giving yields many returns to both the giver and the receiver once they understand the dynamics of giving. Failure to understand this may be a sign that love is still a conditional experience on the part of one or both partners. Or it may show that love is still being used as a means, not as an end.

From Personal Growth to Interdependence

Caring love moves inside a closed circle. It causes the giving and receiving relationships to revolve around each other. Some illustrations:

—A teacher who knows how to learn from the students discovers that the mutual learning creates a bond of mutual respect. The teacher-student relationship becomes deeper than any one-way exchange of information.

—An actor who goes beyond the portrayal of a character to reach deeply into the sensitivities of the audience, and elicits a response from them so powerful and moving that the actor becomes an audience to the response.

—A counselor who heals those who come for help receives affirmation of the effectiveness of the counseling efforts. The counselor's personal satisfaction amounts to a reciprocal form of healing.

This mutuality of healing and being healed produces a circular response of giving and receiving. The teacher, the actor, the counselor discover that by giving without expecting anything in return, they receive something far greater than they gave, something not attainable through any manipulative technique.

In Stage Five consciousness, love as an act of giving without conditions represents the highest stage of character development. It implies the overcoming of dependency, of narcissism, of exploitation, of hoarding, of anything that indicates a person is afraid to trust others through self-giving.

Victory Over Competitiveness

Caring is not competitive. My caring is neither more effective nor more important than your caring. To state the problem that way shows the absurdity of it. What is more important is that you be able to care, and that I be able to care, and that we each have something and someone to care for. Caring also means that I don't have to avoid or resent my own limitations. Neither do I have to hide or explain away my strengths. Caring enables me to accept my own strengths and my own weaknesses; to accept the strengths and the weaknesses of others with balance and equanimity.

Even the unpleasant, painful, intolerable facts that I discern about the other person I must learn to accept with compassion and with understanding. In *agape* loving we can get past roles and conventions, ideals, and goals. We can accept in each other those aspects that seem threatening or painful or embarrassing to both of us. We no longer need to be co-conspirators regarding "things we agree not to talk about." True caring challenges me to become less interested in proving that I am right and the other person is wrong, even though competitive love has been endemic to all my earlier stages. Uncompetitive love lets me become more interested in determining whether what I do in any given situation helps or hinders. It is a way of allowing me finally to become objective about my subjective feelings.

Trust that Energizes

Trust takes on a new dimension when agape love becomes the stage in which we live. To realize that a person trusts me has its own way of activating my feelings for the person I care for. *Agape* has its own way of activating me when I come to understand that a person trusts me. It has a way of activating the other person when I return the trust.

One sign of a lack of trust is my unwillingness to allow the person I love to make mistakes. I require guarantees. I attempt to force him or her into a mold. I overprotect in a way that threatens independence. It's a matter of understanding that other persons have their own problems with wills to break and with behavioral patterns to modify. They don't need, and cannot use, my help.

Trust enables me to allow a person to make mistakes in my presence. It allows me to make mistakes in the presence of the other person. Trust, therefore, involves providing assistance and encouragement. It involves being sensitive to what another person regards as a creative experience. It helps me to avoid forcing myself unduly into the other person's life. Trust allows me to learn from my own mistakes in the relationship without either repeating those mistakes or allowing those mistakes to destroy the relationship. Trust also involves developing a sense of judgment. It involves fine tuning of our communication, so that we come nearer expressing appropriate behavior in our relationship—even in our mistakes.

Humility that Refreshes

In *agape* love, humility also takes on a new meaning. We come to realize that there is always something more to learn about a person. There is always something new and refreshing to learn about behavior, about feelings, about the unconscious motivations that well up within a person. In Stage Five, the opposite of humility is the kind of pride that expresses itself in taking the other person for granted. Pride leads me to stereotype a person's behavior and motives. It leads me to label him or her without due concern for unconscious motives that may be hidden from me. The sin of pride is to say to or about the other person, "I can read her like a book."

A Selfless Form of Self-Centeredness

Caring then creates a new blend of selfless self-centeredness. In this new stage, it is possible to transcend both self denial and its moral opposite, selfishness.

130

In earlier stages, self-denial was upheld as an ideal and also feared as a threat to the ego. Selfishness was forbidden as a moral evil, and also practiced as a way to deal with insecurity. Now, however, the war between self-denial and selfishness can come to an end.

Agape love makes it possible for us to care deeply about ourselves. It means being able to view ourselves from the inside just as we appear from the outside. We begin to see that what people call "selfishness" is just a preoccupation with whether others admire us. Selfish persons actually avoid looking carefully at themselves. They are centrally concerned with whether they can convince themselves that others admire them. They are in fact indifferent to their own growth. If they were more truly committed to growing into a fully centered self, their so-called selfishness would fall away.

In Stage Five, the distinction between selfishness and selflessness now becomes irrelevant. Self-denial is no longer feared as a threat to the ego, nor is it resented as an instrument others use to urge me to do what they want. At the same time, selfishness is no longer an embarrassment that hinders me from acting spontaneously. And it is no longer a guilt-producing test of what is moral. We come to realize that when self-denial is elevated to the highest value, we become preoccupied with selflessness, and we paradoxically fail to reach our aim.

What is more important than the selfish and the selfless is what comes out of the synthesis of the two. In this new synthesis, we can become both more self-critical and more self-affirming. We can become more self-critical if we keep up a steady stream of self-affirmative experiences. And we can become more self-affirming only by learning something new occasionally through self-criticism.

What emerges, then, is an interdependence of two persons who have lost track of the difference between selfishness and selflessness—and have found a new, powerful, satisfying level of intimacy.

From Knowledge to Mystery

Stage Five is as concerned with awe and wonder as it is with knowledge. *Agape* love is to be contrasted with the experimental basis for love that is common in Stage Four. Where experiments take place, one often has to destroy in order to know. With the scientific method, one must dissect the subject in order to analyze it. The experimenter must stop the process in order to study it. The observer must break down living chains in order to understand how they work. In contrast, Stage Five knowledge accepts, absorbs, and transcends experimental knowledge. Stage Five knowledge moves closer to the essence of human existence.

The need to experiment or to destroy is questioned in Stage Five. It is seen as an act of desperation at worst, mere curiosity at best. The more desperate one's need for love, the more likely it is that one will resort to destroying to achieve it. The experimental approach to love represents a lingering *need* for love rather than a free expression of it. In *agape* love my desire to know another person is both kindled and stilled by our union. In *agape* love the need to know is not insatiable. It's not information about the other person's body or mind that is needed. It is the awareness that in *agape* love I know everything and nothing about the other person.

Beyond the Search for Love Objects

The conventional assumption in our society is that love is caused by what is inherent in the person who is loved. Love is thought to be based on mutual attraction. A person seeking conventional love approaches the task like a would-be artist who believes that if he can find just the right sunset or the right still life arrangement, then he will be able to paint beautifully. This is the romantic theory of painting. Modern art has largely moved on to more satisfying approaches to aesthetics, though public taste remains attracted to "what looks pretty," or what instills nostalgia for memories of experiences.

The romantic theory of seeking the proper love object is also still alive and well. It has dominated American culture because it has won out over the ancient custom of arranged marriage. The search for the "right person" often ends in failure, however, leading many persons into a lifelong search involving one partner after another. "Serial marriage" is what the experts call the phenomenon in which people are married to several persons during a lifetime, each marriage ending in divorce. In terms of stage theory, serial marriage is founded upon adolescent consciousness. It

132

is the importation of the dating and courtship cycle into the marriage relationship itself. Life becomes one "steady" relationship after another.

From Revolution to Devotion

To love in the *agape* sense means that we can love wholeheartedly. We can love others as we love each other. We can learn the secret of loving the whole world. We can love life. In our relationship with each other, we have grasped the experience of the other's mystery and ultimate unknowability. We come to realize that all of life and all knowledge lead ultimately to mystery. Therefore, there is no reason to go on an endless search for one person after another as though they were beautiful objects, the possession of which could transform love into something truly meaningful. In contrast, *agape* love comes from the awareness that love emerges out of my depth over to the depth within the other person.

One dimension of caring that is almost entirely unique to the fifth stage is that of devotion. Devotion to another person involves committing ourselves to each other for an unforeseeable future. It involves risk, courage, danger, and ultimately, growth. Through devotion, caring acquires a particular character in Stage Five. It develops the process of overcoming obstacles to a new and radical level. It develops the capacity to keep on in the face of difficulties, particularly when they threaten to destroy the relationship.

The key, once again, is to realize that a crisis in a marriage is usually a signal that the couple is about to cross a boundary to a new stage. By Stage Five, we have crossed the boundary so often we are not threatened by crises anymore. Now we can view the pain and terror and uncertainty as liberating forces. In caring, therefore, we need not experience responsibilities as mere necessary evils. They are responses that come from devotion. They can be accepted with the same sense of anticipation in Stage Five as were the experiences of falling in love back in Stage One.

Caring love helps each of us to grow in our own time and our own way. Time, therefore, becomes a gift that we give each other. The meaning of "patience" is transformed through caring. It no longer means "doing nothing" or "waiting for something to happen." Patience becomes an active process of tactical withdrawal in order that growth may take place. Nurturing personal growth is like nurturing a plant. It requires withdrawal from positive action to allow natural processes to unfold.

Patience is a special kind of participating. It is a way of giving time and giving space to one another. Patience is a special kind of listening to, or being present for, each other. It is a way of enlarging our partner's environment. It's a way of appreciating the amount of confusion and floundering that each of us may need to go through. Through patience we recognize the other person's need for balance and for a chance to gain perspective. As lovers we will give the beloved a time and a space and a chance.

From Equality to Transcendence

Unlike the forms of loving that are appropriate to earlier stages, caring centers in specific persons. Even as late as Stage Four people find it hard to care for specific individuals. That is because love translated into justice expresses itself initially as compassion for groups or classes of underprivileged. Acts done on behalf of individuals appear statistically insignificant, socially inefficient, even unfair to those who are left out. The effect of loving "the masses" ultimately is to reduce justice to the process of dividing an ever smaller resource among a steadily growing number of victims. *Agape*, by contrast, provides the transcendent resource that needs to be injected into social justice if it is to increase rather than decrease the dignity of the individual. Caring in the sense of *agape* makes it possible, permissible, and desirable for each of us to relate compassionately in the name of justice to a single person. *Agape* makes possible the kind of personal commitment and selflessness that is required for becoming a lifelong worker for social justice.

Gaining Control over Sacrifice

Agape enables me to sacrifice what needs to be sacrificed and to treasure what needs to be treasured. This kind of caring enables one to discover that not all sacrifice is worthy. We quite often make sacrifices of what is valuable to us while holding on to the less valuable. A true sacrifice would be to discover what it is that we need to hold on to and what it is that we need to give up, and to give up those things that are not worth keeping. A person can spend a night watching TV, sacrificing the opportunity for intimate conversation. Someone might give up an evening in a place where a deep and meaningful relationship could unfold in order to spend time in a crowded, noisy bar. We make such sacrifices all the time without realizing it.

In Stage Five we come to understand there is no escaping sacrifice, that it is up to us to choose what kind of sacrifice we will make. We will sacrifice the night in the bar, or the night watching television, in pursuit of a higher pleasure. This paradoxical blend of pleasure and sacrifice is quite perplexing to those in the earlier stages where the concept of sacrifice means to give up something that hurts. People are thus conditioned to turn away from a relationship that involves pain and conflict—to sacrifice the greater pleasure for the lesser. Since these traditional concepts of sacrifice appear to emphasize self-denial, they reinforce life on a downward spiral of the less and less satisfying, the less and less meaningful. Once a person makes the connection between sacrifice and higher values, it becomes possible to shake off the years wasted in denial of one's self and the selves of others. Only then can self-transcendent *agape* love become a center for a relationship.

Trusting intimacy allows two people to accept the many contradictions and conflicts within themselves and within the relationship. It allows two persons to affirm the problems instead of fighting over them or retreating from them. The power to do this comes from the development of a pluralistic world view. A person comes to accept as truth that which one affirms from his own perspective, and to accept as another truth that which comes from the other partner's perspective, even though it conflicts with one's own truth. A person comes to accept a third kind of truth, that which is revealed from inside the relationship itself, from the "life of its own." This pluralistic consciousness enables a couple to see how the whole is greater than the sum of its parts—that the relationship is greater than the sum of the lives of the two partners—without taking anything away from the personal growth of each partner.

Safe to Live Dangerously

At this new depth, it is safe at last to acknowledge that one's closest friend and most intimate companion is also the one to

135

whom one is most dangerously vulnerable. In earlier stages, the threat of the intimate enemy is either denied or opposed (flight or fight). In Stage Five, we let the enemy in. We are enabled to grasp the full impact of the other person, not just the "good parts." That sets up the possibility for a new advance together. There is something redemptive about unconditional acceptance. Unconditional does not mean "I accept you unconditionally in order that the offensive aspects of you will go away." It means "I accept you even though I know you have more power to hurt me than anyone else I know. I don't know whether you have the power to resist using your power over me. I don't know whether our trust in each other is a means of letting our guard down and letting in something terrible. Still, I want to let you into my life completely."

Unconditional love can emerge only under conditions of absolute vulnerability. Anything less than vulnerability can create lesser forms of love but not its unconditional expression. Unconditional love makes possible the letting down of the final barriers, the canceling of the final denials, the beginning of the final affirmations possible in a human relationship. Because Stage Five enables us to accept paradox and pluralism, it enables us to go back and recover the earlier stages that are still alive and well within us. For they certainly have remained with us, just as the core of a tree remains within it as it acquires its outer rings.

We have found that it has been necessary to turn away from each preceding stage as we have moved on to each successive stage. In Stage Five, however, we are enabled to take a close look at ourselves and to see the traces of what we still are at times: savage animals, dependent infants, legalistic nit-pickers, anti-sexual spiritual fanatics, insatiable sexual adolescents, manipulative power-seekers, and all the rest. But instead of turning in horror from our perceptions, this time we realize these are precisely the admissions and affirmations on which we can build a deeper relationship than ever. Years of denial and refusal to talk about and feel through our own past histories can give way to passionate unconditional love—or it can spell the end of the journey in an emergency bailout.

Once a couple give themselves to the forces of unconditional love, anything less will destroy the relationship, not simply set it back to an earlier stage. Once one experiences unconditional

136

love, conditional love becomes its opposite, not just its forebear. *Agape* is the ultimate pleasure—and the ultimate danger.

Unconditional love is qualitatively different. Its whole-heartedness creates a new dimension for devotion and communion. It produces the awareness that I know everything—and nothing—about the other person. When our desire for each other is simultaneously kindled and stilled, we are carried to the boundaries between knowledge and mystery. On this boundary, to love with abandon and to love with constancy become one and the same.

Exploring Stage Five Relationships

In the later years of marriage, forces that earlier seemed threatening or mutually exclusive can begin to surface. As the conflicting dynamics begin to resolve themselves, they begin to work together for the good of the relationship and for the growth of each partner. One test of the growth of intimacy is the degree to which previously "unmentionable" subjects work their way into depth communication.

The questions listed below are typical of those that couples find painful or difficult to discuss with positive results before the relationship has matured into the fifth stage.

1. What is the biggest sacrifice your partner has made for the sake of your marriage? After you have shared your answers with each other, let each tell the other what you feel is the greatest sacrifice you have made. Discuss the differences (or similarities) in your perspectives of who is sacrificing what.

2. What is the most courageous act each of you has performed to strengthen or even save your marriage? Share your feelings about these acts of courage.

3. What are the biggest risks each of you has taken that jeopardized your relationship? How has each of you acted to overcome the consequences of these risky acts? Are these consequences still at work?

4. Share with each other what subjects you find hardest to talk about with each other but still try to discuss. Is there a subject either of you would like to talk about but, when you tried, have found your spouse uncooperative? Is there a subject you know you don't even want to talk about? (It isn't necessary to

share these, but the amount of time it takes before you can do so might be a measure of the growth of your relationship.)

5. Are there any areas in your partner's life where you once hoped you would see some change, but no longer expect to see any? How do you account for the cessation of your hopes? Do you feel angry, bitter, resigned—or can you accept what used to be unacceptable?

6. Discuss how each of you feels about letting your partner be wrong. Do you argue with each other óver details? Correct each other in public (however politely) as to the facts of a story one of you is telling? Do you get a sense of satisfaction when you catch each other in mistakes? Think of any recent examples and share your feelings about your need to be right.

7. What is the longest talk you've ever had? Was it about one subject or many? Was it caused by a crisis or did you seek out time together? Was it an argument or a period of shared intimacy? Discuss how you would react if you were to spend tomorrow, the entire twenty-four-hour day, with each other. There would be no TV, nothing to read, no work to do. Just twenty-four hours of time alone together.

8. Discuss two areas where conditional love still affects your marriage. Each of you might try to surface one thing your spouse deeply wants you to do, which you do not want to do under any conditions. Are these the problem areas you would mention? Try to imagine the worst thing that would happen if you broke down and did what your partner wants.

9. What does each of you feel are the biggest threats to the growth or survival of your marriage? What are the resources you could draw on to subdue the threats?

10. What are the most deeply held beliefs or attitudes on which there is the most disagreement between you? When you deal with them, do you try to change each other? Fight for your right to be different? Try to understand each other? In what ways could these differences strengthen your relationship instead of threatening it?

138

Selected Reading for Background and Discussion

Stage Five

Paradox, Reconciliation, and Interdependency

Erich Fromm, *The Art of Loving*
Milton Mayerhoff, *On Caring*
Peter Kreeft, *Love Is Stronger than Death*
Richard Foster, *Celebration of Discipline*
Paul Tillich, *Love, Power, and Justice*
B. D. Napier, *Come, Sweet Death*
John Macquarrie, *Twentieth Century Religious Thought*
Abingdon Dictionary of Living Religions
Karl Barth, *Evangelical Theology: An Introduction*
Martin Luther King, Jr., *Strength to Love*

Stage Six: *Ktisis,*
Creative Love Beyond Boundaries

Every era has to reinvent
the project of "spirituality" for itself.
(Spirituality = plans, terminologies,
ideas of deportment
aimed at resolving
the painful structural contradictions
inherent in the human situation,
at the completion of human consciousness,
at transcendence.)
         —Susan Sontag, *The Aesthetics of Silence*[11]

[The extermination camp prisoners who survived]
came to realize that they still retained . . .
the last, if not the greatest, of the human freedoms:
to choose their own attitude
in any given circumstance.
         —Bruno Bettelheim, *The Informed Heart*[12]

Great discoveries have in the past been made
by survivors—of dying historical epochs as well
as of actual catastrophes. . . .

Our present difficulty is
that we can no longer be sure
of this opportunity.

We can no longer count upon
survivor wisdom
deriving from weapons
which are without limit
in what they destroy.
—Robert Jay Lifton, *Death in Life: Survivors of Hiroshima*[13]

For the smallest building blocks of matter,
every process of observation
creates a disturbance. . . .
We can no longer talk
of the behavior of the particle
apart from the process of observation. . . .
We must become aware of the fact that . . .
we are not only spectators
but also always participants
on the stage of life.
—Warner Heisenberg, *Nature in Contemporary Physics*[14]

There remains one more "divorce" that can be traced to its
psychological and cultural roots. It is the hardest one of all to
describe because, unlike the other divorces of a healthy marriage,
the fifth one affects each relationship differently.

Simply put, the fifth divorce breaks a couple away from all
the norms and roles and styles of relationships they see around
them, including those of other couples of their acquaintance who
have made it into Stage Five. Stage Six introduces a no-man's
land, a *u-topos*, where the couple must live without the support
of any cultural and psychological resources from their environment. They are on their own. They are pioneers, innovators,
creators in the realm of relationships.

Unless a couple can survive in such an atmosphere Stage Six
will be closed to them. When they are faced with these kinds of
boundary conditions, some couples draw back because they cannot live without a plan. Others wander across the boundary
unthinkingly and become lost in an aimless course. But couples
who survive and thrive and flourish in Stage Six will be drawing
upon an invisible sense of purpose. They will have learned how to
live in hope when the signs of progress are absent and not to
despair, rage, or destroy the fragile bridges back to previous
stages.

By definition Stage Six is the kind of world where basic trust is carried to its ultimate, where we see only in part and not the whole, where we walk by faith and not by sight, where we go out not knowing where we are going, journeying toward the land of promise.

The Sources of Stage Six Loving

Since there are no resources to draw upon from one's own personality development, or from cultural forces around us, where does a couple go to find guidance for growth in Stage Six? There is an analogy that is common to all of us, and that is the experience of one's own death. To reflect on the experience of death provides a meaningful way to understand life without roots, without precedence, without limits.

The distinction between the experience of dying and the experience of death is crucial here. Unlike my experience of dying, my death cannot be done well or poorly. I may be able to leave behind a heroic or uplifting example of how to die, but my death itself will be neither cowardly nor brave. Dying is the focus and wellspring of great religious insight and devotion throughout history. The event of death itself, however, by its very definition admits of no knowledge apart from that of the one dying.

The great theologians and psychologists reflect awareness of this distinction between dying and death. The most profound devotional and mystical writings are able to bring a person into contemplation of the mystery of death. There have always been those escape artists, however, who have wanted to lead us away from mystery into something more sensational by providing accounts of out-of-body experiences, messages from beyond the grave, and assertion of special psychic powers. These attempts merely blur the communicable process of dying and the existential experience of one's own death.

Those who are willing to face their dying faithfully and heroically must also be willing to face their own death as the ultimate incommunicable experience. For these the possibility of a Stage Six consciousness lies just across the horizon.

Learning to Live with the Unprecedented

Once we have come to understand this distinction between dying and death, our life in the world takes on a new perspective.

142

Life itself comes to be seen as a series of unprecedented events. Human history can be viewed as a series of creative and original events. Our individual lives are treasuries of first-time experiences still accessible to us: the first sense of touch, the first heartbeat, the first breath, the first cry, the first step, the first word. Most of us do not reflect fully on our powers of originality and therefore do not use them to the fullest. So we find ourselves facing the boundary between Stage Five and Stage Six unaware of our resources.

Any parent who has tried to observe a baby's first step or first word knows how difficult and even infuriating the watch can be. The process is so gradual! Who can say when a particular leg motion is a true step and when a particular babble of sound is a true word?

Human beings have never been ready for change. We have preferred to describe change with terms that emphasize continuity, terms such as flow, process, evolution, or revolution. Of course these terms refer to the speed of change, to its smoothness or its relative predictability, while ignoring the shock of the truly new. In an utterly new world, there are no rules. In such a world, the crisis is an ultimate one, going to the heart of basic trust. Some will decide that religion does not have the best interests of human beings at heart and that what it forbids—murder, lying, adultery—are permissible. Others, however, peer into the paradox of the truly new and realize that the deepest faith in God is to hold to human values even if God does not exist. Such people realize that, even if the idea of God were nothing more than a human construct, the question becomes whether or not this human idea is a positive one. The issue becomes one of humankind's basic capacity for trust.

In order to live in Stage Six, one must firmly grasp both poles of a paradox and realize that there is a way of overcoming conflicts, such as that between traditional theism and atheism, in terms of our ability to experience the unconditional, the truly new.

The Supreme Test of Faithfulness

To live in Stage Six means that I will love my spouse, that I will be faithful, but not out of fear of divine penalty or out of imitation of a divine personality. Love in Stage Six requires that I

143

see the value of faithfulness even if faithlessness has no consequences. This is the supreme test of character: To trust that commitment can become the ultimate pleasure principle. And yet a Stage Six couple sees the infinite potential of an intimate relationship and pursues it for its own sake. Stage Six love means that intimacy is granted in the very nature of human consciousness.

Marriage in our time offers the opportunity for a breathtaking variety of new styles and new levels of experience. Only a few couples, however, will take the risks and make the sacrifices to discover the full potential of their relationship. Those who do so will be able to draw upon the creative activities and the enjoyment of being original in their personal lives. They will be able to draw upon the cultural resources of the creative breakthroughs scattered with such abandon throughout history. These are resources that make Stage Six so compelling.

As we look more closely at the characterization of love in Stage Six, it is appropriate again to suggest models of relationships that exemplify these characteristics. The purpose of selecting these models is to show that there are in every era individuals who are breaking new ground, who are shaking up the conventional wisdom. To these we are indebted, for without their ventures we could not take for granted the victories they have brought us.

1. Abraham and Sarah: From Paternalism to Promises

In the ancient Near East, the most common form of marriage was the one anthropologists call polygyny—one man with several wives. The origins of this system may go back into the mists of history when the life of the male was one fraught with physical danger, leading to the numerical predominance of women. Such a system, as we noted in an earlier chapter, was a means of continuing traditional values, maintaining blood ties, keeping property ownership stable, and continuing apprenticeship as a way of controlling vocation. Three thousand years ago a new system was emerging, one that anthropologists call conjugal marriage, in which husband and wife would leave their respective families and develop a small family of their own. This was the period to which the biblical story of Abraham and Sarah is attributed. In the conjugal family there developed a new potential for individual mate selection and for the growth of sexual attraction, romantic love, and independence from geographical ties.

One story about Abraham and Sarah centers around Sarah's jealousy of the concubine Hagar, the inevitable tension between the wife who could not have children and the concubine who could. But in this story it turns out that the concubine was banished from the household while the childless wife remained—a twist on the usual preeminence given to childbearing.

Another story describes Abraham's taking his wife away from their ancestral homeland into a land of promise. The story serves as a symbol of moving toward a future in which persons are led by God, who blesses the people not merely by maintaining the ancestral land but by leading them into the unknown.

A third story dramatizes the miracle of Sarah's pregnancy at a late age—a further reinforcement of the relationship between the husband and wife that had continued for decades without the usual binding force of parenthood. In cultures where these stories have been taken seriously, the changes symbolized by the transitions in the lives of Abraham and Sarah are truly decisive for the history of love, for the alternatives available to couples.

2. Mary and Joseph: The Holy Family

The centuries of medieval art portray Mary in a rich and complex manner, making it difficult for us to see the truly revolutionary impact upon marriage that the images of Mary and Joseph have had on Western culture. In the Holy Family we see an ancient sign of the nuclear family replacing the extended family. We see a sign of the breakup of intergenerational continuity. The Holy Family may also be seen as a sign of the breakdown of the sexual and biological family, for the child in this case is not the offspring of the father with the mother. It is perhaps the most famous stepfamily in history. A further wedge against convention is that Joseph raises an adopted boy as though he were Joseph's own, presenting a model of a spiritual relationship within the nuclear relationship.

From a historical perspective, the impact of Mary and Joseph upon the possibilities of love and marriage lies primarily with the spiritualization of that which until then had been primarily biological and economic relationships. Devotion to Mary played a richly complex part in starting Christian culture down a path away from male supremacy. It is interesting to observe, however, that the rise of Mary has had a different impact upon males than upon females. For men in medieval times, devotion to Mary centered upon images of the Queen of Heaven, a source of power, the Virgin, a symbol of purity, and as the Mother of God, a reminder of one's own filial duties. For women, however, a more private and domestic idea arose: Women identified with Mary as one who could be reached, as one who was always accessible. Mary was viewed by women as the virgin who maintained her dignity and identity apart from roles as mother and wife. She was seen as a spiritual sister in whose name spiritual communities of women could live and develop. For female mystics throughout the Middle Ages, Mary served as an ideal prophetess, visionary, and seer.

The role of Joseph in medieval reflection is also quite diverse and many-faceted. The image of St. Joseph has appeared as a symbol of the ideal domestic parent, not only as one who takes care of children he did not help to conceive but as the humble carpenter who apprenticed the Messiah. This became a symbol of the dignity of labor and an earthly sign of the heavenly relationship of father and son. Even in our time the Holy Family exerts a powerful spiritual force. In a time when the breakup of the nuclear family is calling for models where spiritual kinship transcends and replaces biological kinship, the model of Mary, Joseph, and Jesus offers far-reaching, untapped resources for the preservation of family values.

3. *Abelard and Heloise:* Sic et Non *to Passion*

The story of the brash young philosopher and his beautiful teenage lover has fascinated and chilled every generation since the eleventh century. Peter Abelard, the founder of the University of Paris, lived in an era when erotic and spiritual loves lay at opposite, mutually exclusive poles. To envision the experiences of both passion and spiritual love in the context of romance or marriage was both naive and courageous, pioneering yet doomed to failure. Abelard was a brilliant young theologian, both respected and resented by older peers. He fell in love with a beautiful and precocious young woman in one of his classes, and obtained a tutoring position in her home. With Heloise he began a passionate, erotic affair that apparently surprised both of them in its power. Naively, perhaps, they were open about the impact of the relationship on their lives, and historical sources give us accounts of impressions of both. Neither seemed to worry much about being discovered or censured or about the later consequences on marriage or family. There was a blend of physical love in the classical sense along with courtly love in the romantic sense. A unique feature was the public character of their love.

Heloise's uncle, a father figure in this case, is finally told what the whole town knows. The students especially are abuzz, and because of his lack of knowledge the uncle is being made a laughingstock. Humiliated, betrayed, and morally outraged, he arranges a late-night attack in which the young Abelard is brutally castrated.

The reactions of both Heloise and Abelard became as widely known as the affair. Abelard was devastated. He felt he could no longer be Heloise's lover and that his teaching career was in jeopardy. In his anxiety, he made a fateful decision on behalf of both of them, that they would enter the monastic life. He would focus on his teaching, and she would live secluded from public ridicule. After making their romantic vows, Abelard and Heloise had little contact for several years. At length, however, they exchanged a series of letters that revealed their feelings. Heloise had always been willing to live with Abelard as his lover and not burden his teaching career with the duties of marriage. But Abelard first and foremost was a teacher and a servant of the church. He was apparently surprised at the force of their erotic passion, its ability to challenge and overwhelm him in his teaching responsibilities.

The final correspondence between the two shows a heartbroken Heloise, who had been willing to sacrifice everything for love, and an adamant Abelard, who to the end was committed to an intellectual and spiritual life. However famous he became, he never became reconciled to the power of passion.

From the perspective of stage theory, the lasting impact of Abelard and Heloise lies in their courageous though tragic attempt to follow both their passionate and their spiritual impulses. Tragedy ensued because in marriages of their time circumstances were not favorable for both the spiritual and the physical to coexist and mutually enhance each other.

4. *Martin and Katrin Luther: Children, Church and Kitchen*

The ideals of spiritual and physical love were brought together at the time of the Protestant Reformation. The marriage of a former monk, Martin Luther, and a former nun, Katrin von Bora, serves as a symbol of the change. The Reformation taught that marriage and family were a greater "school for character" than celibacy and religious orders.

The early sixteenth century produced a flood of marriages between priests and nuns. These were forced to leave religious orders, but that did not mean they left religious service. Many joined in leading the reforms that brought Protestantism into existence. Martin and Katrin were fitting symbols of this shift. In practice, the marriage of the Luthers produced a rather typical autocratic family structure, not venturing much beyond the convention of *Kinder, Kuche, Kirche*. Even so, the traditional minister's family has developed over the last three centuries as a role model to all families in the community. Indeed, even up to the present the minister's family has been at the forefront in a number of major social issues, from women's rights in the nineteenth century to struggles over ordination in the twentieth.

5. *Robert Browning and Elizabeth Barrett Browning: The Creation of Devotion*

Because the Victorian romantic period is so close to our own time, its impact on us is easily taken for granted. Love as passion lies at the very heart of romantic love. Yet what contemporary society accepts as passion has been much devalued through the popular media over the last several generations. The intensity, terror, and strangeness that were a part of romantic love in the Victorian era have become mere conventions gone stale in our own time.

The romance between Robert Browning and Elizabeth Barrett symbolizes romantic love at its flowering. All the elements are there, in archetypal form: the chance meeting, the initial distance between the two, misunderstandings that lead to distrust, unfavorable circumstances that prevented their getting close to each other, the dramatic moment when barriers fall and they come to see that they are in love. All these forces that now are clichés for Hollywood-style fiction kindled in the romance of Robert and Elizabeth, one of literature's most interesting and compelling loves.

In her twenties Elizabeth Barrett was an invalid, kept at home by a tyrannical father who had forbidden all his children to marry. A former slaveholder in Jamaica before the British emancipation, Mr. Barrett exercised a power over his daughter and her siblings that is all but unimaginable today. Elizabeth's life was in her mind, existing only through her reading of the classics, a world that formed the basis of her poetry. Even at an early age she revealed in her verse a depth and tenderness, an innocence and sophistication that were held together by her genius.

In his youth Robert Browning was also a writer of poetry that had drawn some attention. But its dense, mystical, unmusical cadence made it decidedly out of favor in an age immersed in Wordsworth, Byron, and Tennyson. Some of his poetry fell into the hands of Elizabeth, however. Unlike most of his readers, she was able to comprehend and appreciate its complexities. She let some of their mutual contacts know of her interest. One mutual friend told Robert about her and also shared some of her writings with him.

It is said that Robert Browning first fell in love with the poetry and then with the poetess. Immediately upon being smitten, he sent her a passionate letter in which his own control over the English language was taxed to the fullest as he tried to conceal his desire to meet her, to visit her and to come to know her. When Elizabeth received the letter, her first response was one of terror, partly because of her physical disabilities and because she knew that a relationship with anyone but her ever-watchful father was doomed to failure. Nevertheless, she wrote a letter in return, thinly disguising her own excitement at the possibility of their meeting. More letters flurried back and forth over a period of several months before they finally met. During this time of delay, Elizabeth's physical condition began to improve dramatically and (to the household) mysteriously until, by the time she met Robert for the first time (a closely guarded secret, of course), she was no longer confined to her house but was able to travel with him. Their marriage followed a few weeks after their first meeting. It was an elopement filled with suspense. They formed an elaborate scheme to marry and leave the country before her father could find out.

They settled in Italy, where Elizabeth and Robert spent their time writing together while living in a series of villas in the mountains and by the sea. There they discovered the classical world was still alive, and for the twelve years they spent together they created some of the greatest poetry of their generation.

Theirs was truly a relationship in which each was the creative wellspring for the other. Robert was completely unthreatened by Elizabeth's fame, popularity, and brilliance. In fact, these were the forces that attracted him to her. In return he found perhaps the only person alive who was brilliant enough to understand his depths and who possessed the caring passion to keep him writing in spite of his continued rejection by the literate public of the day.

Elizabeth died in 1861, and Robert lived until 1889. What history owes to their twelve brief years of marriage was a love that bordered on and drew its inspiration from the sacred. The imagery of their letters to each other and the allusions to love in their writings drew heavily on religious and spiritual symbolism. Their feelings for each other were described in the language of adoration, glorification, and devotion. The Brownings lived in a time when the sense of the transcendent was undergoing great transition. Industrial development was transforming the countryside, making life easier for the poor but also spreading uglinesss in its wake. Democratic revolutions were destroying empires and giving birth to the possibility of freedom, while at the same time introducing new depths of brutality and violence into the farthest reaches of European society. The romantic energies inspired by this revolution are reflected in the lives of these two poets who in their writings left a permanent (they would say eternal) legacy.

The Search for Heroic Love in America Today
Someone has said that the lives of medieval saints are better admired than imitated. That is an aspect of hero worship that Americans seem to recognize about loving couples, if the personality features of popular magazines are indicative. Americans accept their "ideal couples" for their ability to add spice and seasoning to life. If pressed, we would seldom be willing to trade places with the celebrities we admire. Fame, we suppose, is a nice place to visit, but we wouldn't want to live there. Americans seem to be not so concerned about private successes or failures; it is the

150

myth-engendering capabilities of our love heroes that are more important to the discussion at hand.

On the following pages are studies of three famous American couples chosen to represent different value systems and different parts of our culture. These studies deal with the public perception of the achievements of the couples rather than with their own private experiences.

Paul Newman and Joanne Woodward: Lovers of High Risk
Here is a couple that seems to blend the qualities of celebrity, talent, equality, and sexuality. They symbolize the elements of high risk: a man whom millions consider one of the most attractive men alive, married to a woman acknowledged to be extraordinarily gifted, beautiful, intelligent, and perceptive.

Counter to these widely acknowledged feelings are another more contradictory set. Millions of women who admire Joanne Woodward fantasize being with Paul Newman, while American men have somewhat different but equally contradictory attitudes about the couple.

"She's not good enough for him."

"How I'd like to trade places with her just once!"

"How does she keep him, with all those other women around?"

"I wonder how she handles the way other women feel about him? He'd have to be a fool not to take advantage of the opportunities."

"Poor Joanne. I wonder if she's covering up her real feelings. She's probably a tough lady."

"She probably fools around a lot."

"Who knows, though? He may actually take good care of her. After all, she has homes on both coasts and the financial security to pick only the films she wants."

Such reflections about Paul and Joanne as individuals lead to an even deeper curiosity about their relationship:

"I wonder if she resents putting her career second to his."

"I wonder if she resents having to take a larger share of their family life."

"I wonder how much she owes her talent to him. After all, he produced and directed some of her most unusual and difficult roles."

151

"But you know, the roles he produced showed her in most unflattering ways. I wonder if that's courage or insecurity on his part."

"Maybe he feels guilty about the way he treats her and that's why he backs her films."

"Then again, maybe he couldn't be the superstar he is without her support and sacrifice."

And so it goes. These are questions that continue to tease the minds of millions of fans, and yet they have never been answered satisfactorily. This is partly because questions like these never result in ultimate answers. All they can do is open areas for further questioning and speculation. The popular press will continue to probe these issues but will always fail to satisfy public curiosity.

It seems to be the function of a marriage like that of Paul Newman and Joanne Woodward to provide an ideal model for American culture. It challenges us to blend sex appeal with long-term commitment, to develop talent along with a stable home life, to devote ourselves to family and also to controversial public causes. Each of these is a value we treasure, and each is a value difficult to acquire. In the case of this couple, however, it all seems to work.

Someday, some reporter may come out with the "real story," an account of the Newman-Woodward relationship that will contradict the public image of the last twenty years. Even if that should happen, it may not even have an effect on people's feelings about the couple. Certainly it would not remove the lasting, positive impact this marriage has had on countless other couples who have been struggling with, and trying to juggle, one or more of the sets of challenges that, to their credit, we associate with Paul Newman and Joanne Woodward.

Roy Rogers and Dale Evans: King of the Cowboys, Queen of the West
For more than forty years now, the marriage of Roy Rogers and Dale Evans has provided a near-perfect case study of how American legends are created. They arrived on the scene just as Hollywood was mining the lingering memories of the settlement

of the West for its romantic, heroic ideals. Here was a young woman who as a teenager ran away from her home in Texas to be a blues singer in Chicago nightclubs. She had a past to hide, a son whom she called her little brother. In Hollywood she met a young man who had been born upstairs over a store in a small town in Ohio but who had listened to faraway radio stations and dreamed of being a country and western singer. They met in Hollywood and became a screen couple in "B" Western movies. Then they became a married couple, and finally that couple became a legend.

It's difficult now to recapture the near-total saturation of Dale Evans and Roy Rogers as role models for a whole generation of pre-television American children. During the 1940s, millions of children learned to walk, talk, act, dress, and sing like Roy and Dale. They carried their school lunches in Roy and Dale lunch pails. Radio, motion pictures, comic books, clothing, accessories, foods—almost anything that touched the lives of children bore the stamp of Roy and Dale. Saturday-afternoon movie matinees featuring the couple were a weekly ritual in small towns across America.

Then during the 1950s, with the advent of TV, something happened to American popular culture. The capacity for total saturation with heroes and their adoring women underwent a change. A vastly different role model emerged—the model of the antihero, a rebel and outlaw standing against society. James Dean, Elvis, the Beatles, the Rolling Stones created new social conventions, a new definition of the self, a new set of values. The new model addressed a new set of problems for which the older prescriptions of love and optimism, of generosity, of compassionate helping of the helpless seemed shallow and inadequate to meet new and increasingly desperate needs.

Today our culture seems to view Roy Rogers and Dale Evans as figures of camp, of nostalgia mixed with contempt. And yet, there is something alongside this camp view that haunts us as we mourn for a lost age of innocence. Our antiheroes have lived out in their private lives the self-destructive impulses that they express in their stage personae. In the meantime, Roy Rogers and Dale Evans have lived out the quiet heroism that they urged upon their youthful admirers. Their devotion to the cause of children has continued. In their own home they have brought up a dozen

153

foster children and have experienced the tragic death of three of their children. They have given countless hours and have traveled many miles to hold benefits for children's hospitals and for research on children's diseases. And long before the subject came to its present public awareness, the problem of child abuse had been their concern.

Today at the occasional public appearance of Roy Rogers or Dale Evans, they evoke what seems to be a renewed respect on the part of the public. It's as though people want to feel that they have outgrown their childhood innocence, and yet they wonder who really has come along to blaze happier trails than the King of the Cowboys and the Queen of the West. . . .

Martin Luther King, Jr. and Coretta Scott King: Can Love Transcend Death?

The Brownings treated their marriage as an eternal bond of adoration, and added depth and intensity to their love. Martin Luther King and Coretta Scott King represent a different way of transcending death in a marriage—the way of commitment to a dream and a movement.

Their marriage started with some traditional trappings. He was a Protestant minister, and she had a singing career that she submerged in order to carry out roles as wife and mother. But as the civil rights movement progressed, Dr. King found himself working more and more outside the boundaries of the conventional clergy role. And Mrs. King found that her talents as a singer were even more in demand as a rallying force for the movement.

Did the dream die with the dreamer? From a strictly historical point of view, some would say that the dream was already in decline before the assassination of Dr. King. And yet a decade and a half of perspective has clarified the undying aspects of the dream: integration of public facilities, the rise of hundreds of black political leaders and office-holders, the many awards and honors and holidays commemorating the name of Martin Luther King, Jr.

As a force in her own right, Mrs. King must be reckoned with today by those who seek the blessing of the Black leadership in America. Respect for her late husband is one element of her moral force, but an even more vibrant element is her own ability to symbolize the aspirations of Black Americans and of women in this country and around the world. The kind of love preached and practiced by Dr. King was bound up with what he called redemptive undeserved suffering. The life of Coretta Scott King has been the focal point for an extraordinary share of undeserved suffering. That such experience has proved redemptive to others is not an automatic result of the suffering itself; it is the outcome of her own commitment to nonviolent resistance to evil. It may be true that no greater love can be shown than to lay down one's life for one's friends. It is also true that to honor one who has laid down his life, living out the dream of that individual is a form of the greatest love.

The Next Pioneers of Loving

And where do we go from here? To a future with still more challenges than the present. Even now we feel our relationships being drawn along into the future. We look around us and realize that the most common form of marriage of just a generation ago—that of two teenagers with one or two years of high school—has become the least stable, having the highest divorce rate. The cultural supports for this form of marriage are fast eroding in urban technological America. The same process gives every sign of eating past the edges of today's college-educated, two-career, having-it-all marriages. At the same time it seems equally clear that the future does not lie in the direction of the more experimental lifestyles of recent years—open marriage, homosexual relationships, communal marriage. All such experiences involve extending the intimacies of marriage into other types of relationships.

The true pioneering breakthroughs in consciousness and understanding will be achieved, I believe, in the one-man, one-woman relationship. It is still the simplest and quickest way that advances in intimacy can develop. Other types of relationships will progress by applying the discoveries of monogamy to their own areas. Ultimately, all relationships seem to depend on the monogamous one for pioneering discoveries. Indeed, the arrangements popularized in so much of our futuristic literature come from Stage Four adolescent experimenting with lifestyles and value systems, not from a new stage in the historic adventure of discovering new depths of intimacy.

155

Here is the challenge and adventure that lies open before individuals who are willing to do what is necessary to develop a Stage Six consciousness:

—To engage in spending and being spent in order to transform present reality into a transcendent reality.

—To develop a vivid taste and feel for transcendence and for its extraordinary and unpredictable qualities.

—To be heedless of the personal threats of pioneering, in order to become a disciplined activist incarnating love and justice.

And so what the future holds depends on the answer we give to a question about ultimate commitment: whether we can believe that love is more powerful than death.

Commitment to love as the ultimate value involves exploration and adventure through the stages introduced in this book. Commitment to love is based on faith that love is the ultimate value. We can say that God is love and that love is God only as long as we keep in mind that our experience of love at any time is limited, and that at no time can we apprehend the totality of love.

So our choice must reach beyond our experience, and it may come down ultimately to our capacity to trust that love is stronger than death. Some forms of love are not stronger than death and, as we have seen, they give way to other forms of love; they die. But the future of human loving lies in the hearts of those who do believe that in some ultimate way what they have experienced is more powerful than the death they have yet to experience. Those who cannot bring themselves to such a belief will allow death to triumph over love in their hearts. And if death can defeat love, there is nothing to prevent it from becoming the destroyer of all our other values as well.

The future of love lies with those who can see beyond the rest of us, those who can envision a relationship that is as much of a breakthrough in our understanding as have been the pioneering works of love in the past. In a very real sense, our present enjoyment of loving relationships depends upon the forces bidding us to come and join them in the unknown future at least as much as they depend upon the forces of the past from which we have inherited so much.

What we have left, after this review of the resources available to us for loving, is a keener awareness of the great possibilities that lie before us. If these possibilities appear vague for the moment, they may not always be so. Clarity and concreteness will come as we spend more time in creative loving; they are a result of Stage Six, not a prerequisite. We realize that we discover, again and again, that a new and more satisfying period of equilibrium will always follow a period of difficulty—and that still other new, disorienting learning experiences will follow each period of equilibrium. We are coming to understand that love appears to move around in circles, yet at ever higher planes, in a kind of upward spiral. Perhaps this image of the upward spiral can linger in our minds as a vivid symbol of the evidence of our own experience, that love is ultimately more powerful than death.

Talking Together About Pioneering Love
This is a good place to reflect upon the areas of your life in which you've had to become a pioneer.

1. What are some aspects of your life in which you have had to face new issues that did not exist for your parents?

2. What challenges are the two of you struggling with that, as far as you know, are not problems for any of your friends?

3. As you reflect on these areas where you feel you are going it alone, what resources and approaches have you developed for trying to cope? What things have worked, and what things haven't? See if you can detect any patterns or draw any conclusions about the ways you've succeeded as pioneers.

4. "Pioneer" has a kind of quaint ring about it, seemingly more appropriate to the days of our forefathers and foremothers. And that's intentional. From what you know of your parents and grandparents, what situations did they encounter in which they were the pioneers? In what ways have they perhaps passed on a certain spirit of facing the unknown that you might have inherited? Could you make more use of your inheritance?

5. Here are some typical changes people are struggling with today. Rank them in the order in which they've influenced your life:

—a move to a different culture (rural to urban, urban to rural, another language, a different political system, wartime, etc.).

—a change in economic status (sudden affluence or sudden loss of income, change in vocation, level of responsibility, or job security).

157

—a change in health (serious accident, prolonged illness, development of a chronic condition or permanent handicap).

—a spiritual crisis in which you experienced either a loss of faith, a new discovery of spiritual resources, or both. As you reflect on these changes, try to focus on how you dealt with the areas where no one seemed to understand or to offer helpful counsel. Then see if you can determine the areas of life now where, consciously or unconsciously, you are operating out of discoveries you made in dealing with the unknown.

6. Here are some ways people often fail to cope with the unknown:

—become mentally paralyzed, retreating into fear, insecurity or resentment.

—find one way to cope, then become rigid in applying it to all similar situations.

—follow the advice of others, only to find you are receiving conflicting directions.

—passively accept a painful situation for a long time, then suddenly explode and make a lot of radical, irreversible decisions.

—compulsively try one thing after another, never sticking with one method long enough to see if it works.

When you find yourself recognizing patterns like these in your own life, can you think of any ways to break them, even if it means facing the future without knowing how you will manage?

7. Among the people you know, list those who are able to help you:

—introduce yourself to a wider world in an accepting manner.

—find your unique identity and not expect you to live as they do.

—unify and center your life, not judging yourself or other people for their immaturity or mistakes.

—work on your own life to heal the things you dislike in others.

—take risks on behalf of loving relationships.

If these people are available to you, how could you let them know the importance of their lives for you? And if they're people you've admired from a distance, from books they've written or achievements you admire, how can you continue to be drawn by them into higher expressions of loving?

Selected Reading for Background and Discussion
Stage Six
Creative Love Beyond the Boundaries

John F. Kennedy, *Profiles in Courage*
Paul Tillich, *The Courage to Be*
Rollo May, *The Courage to Create*
Sallie Sears and Georgianna W. Lord, *The Discontinuous Universe: Selected Writings in Contemporary Consciousness*
Albert Rothenberg, *The Emerging Goddess: The Creative Process in Art, Science and Other Fields*
Frederick J. Hoffman, *Imagination's New Beginning: Theology and Modern Literature*
Joel Shor and Jean Ganville, *Illusion in Loving: A Psychoanalytic Approach to the Evolution of Intimacy and Autonomy*
Jessie Bernard, *The Future of Marriage*
Joan Hunt and Richard Hunt, *Growing Love in Christian Marriage: A Couple's Manual*
Mel Krantzler, *Creative Marriage*
Norton F. Kristy, *Staying in Love: Reinventing Marriage and Other Relationships*

And love
Will live its suffering again,
Risk its own defeat again,
Endure the loss of everything again
And yet again and yet again
In doubt, in dread, in ignorance, unanswered.
Over and over, with the dark before,
The dark behind it . . . and still live . . . still love.
THE PLAY IS ENDED

—Archibald MacLeish, *J. B.: A Play in Verse*[15]

Notes

1. Rollo May, *Love and Will*. W. W. Norton, 1969, p. 73.
2. Erich Fromm, *The Art of Loving*. Harper & Row, 1974, p. 53.
3. C. S. Lewis, *The Four Loves*. Harcourt Brace Jovanovich, Inc., 1971, pp. 190-191.
4. Nathaniel Branden, *The Psychology of Romantic Love*. St. Martin's Press, 1981, p. 50.
5. Letha Scanzoni and Mary Hardesty, *All We Were Meant to Be*. Word Books, 1975, pp. 76-77.
6. W. B. Yeats, "Down by the Salley Gardens," in *The Poems of W. B. Yeats*, ed. Robert J. Finneran. Macmillan, 1983, p. 20.
7. David Viscott, *How to Live with Another Person*. Pocket Books, 1983, pp. 19-20.
8. Paul Tillich, *Love, Power, and Justice*. Oxford University Press, 1954, pp. 82-83.
9. Robert Raines, *Living the Questions*, p. 126.
10. Peter Kreeft. *Love Is Stronger than Death*. Harper & Row, 1979, p. 89.
11. Susan Sontag, "The Aesthetics of Silence," in *A Susan Sontag Reader*. Farrar, Straus & Giroux, 1982, p. 181.
12. Bruno Bettelheim, *The Informed Heart*. Macmillan: The Free Press, 1960, p. 158.
13. Robert Jay Lifton, *Death in Life: Survivors of Hiroshima*. University of Chicago Press, 1982, p. 436.
14. Werner Heisenberg, "The Representation of Nature in Contemporary Physics," in *The Discontinuous Universe*. Basic Books, pp. 126-127.
15. Archibald MacLeish, *J. B.: A Play in Verse*. Samuel French, 1958, p. 110.